Creating Business Growth: 21 Successful Marketers Reveal Their Top Business Marketing Secrets

Editor:

Stefan Drew

Contributors:

Stefan Drew
Michael Zipursky
Peter Sandeen
Nick Jervis
Jason "Wally" Waldron
Tom Zeeb
Mike Seddon
Donnie Bryant
Jonathan Altfeld
Bnonn Tennant
Eugene Farber
Meny Hoffman
John Corcoran
Matthew Kimberley
Joseph Bushnell
Steve Gordon
Ian Brodie
Srikumar Rao
Justin Krane
Vernon Riley
Laura Ashley-Timms
Dominic Ashley-Timms

Creating Business Growth: 21 Successful Marketers Reveal Their Top Business Marketing Secrets

Published by Marketing Magician Practical Guides

Cover design © by Mike Seddon
Internal design © by Steve Gordon, Stefan Drew & Lauren Rimes

Marketing Magician Practical Guides
2 Manleys Lane
Dunkeswell
Honiton, Devon EX14 4XQ
United Kingdom

http://www.creatingbusinessgrowth.com

Ordering Information:
Quantity sales. Special discounts are available on quantity purchases by corporations, associations, and others. For details, contact the “Special Sales Department” at the address above.

Creating Business Growth; 21 Successful Marketers Reveal Their Top Business Marketing Secrets/ Stefan Drew –1st ed.

ISBN 978-0-9931623-1-2

Dedication

This book is dedicated to Dov Gordon, Founder of the JVMM Group which all the contributors belong to, because without the JVMM Group many of us would not have met or worked together and this book would not exist.

We all highly recommend his free training on "How to Be Noticed, Be Valued and Be Paid by the Clients You Want Most."

Find it at http://dovgordon.net/bepaid

And for Sharon for her inspiration and love

Contents

Free Resources

At the end of each chapter you can download resources from the person that wrote that chapter. There are some great resources available and you can dig far deeper at no cost.

If you now own this book you are also entitled to register for additional resources. Included are invites to webinars, events and other offers the contributors may make from time to time.

We'll email updates about once a month and will never provide your details to any one else. These updates are also free.

This is how you register:

Go to: http://tinyurl.com/ExtraMarketingResources
and complete the subscription box with your name and email address

Editor's Foreword

Imagine where your business would be if you could tap into the expertise of some of the leading marketing brains available. People who have proven themselves by writing bestsellers. Books that only became bestsellers because the authors put into practice the techniques that they wrote about.

What if some of those people were TED speakers, or had made fortunes for themselves, and their clients, by putting into practice the marketing strategies and tactics they had perfected over years?

Would you, and your business, benefit if you had access to the knowledge these people possess?

With that knowledge, could you realise your dreams?

Stop dreaming.

This is the real world and you have the opportunity to turn your dream into reality.

Twenty-One Leading Authorities

Twenty-one people, all leading authorities in their field of expertise, have joined forces to write a book that could turn your dreams into reality.

These people are based around the globe and have clients on every continent. I'm privileged to know each and every one of these people, because we are all part of the same mastermind group. It's called the Joint Venture Master Mind Group (JVMM) and on monthly calls (and sometimes other mediums) we share our experiences, both good and bad, and so continually improve our strategies, tactics, techniques and profits.

The people in this group are leaders in their fields. They have been specially selected by my friend, Dov Gordon, and Dov imposes strict joining criteria. The main one is that you are exceptionally good at what you do.

Just twenty-one people from the larger JVMM group came together to write this book. The result is probably one of the most inspiring marketing books ever written. It focuses on what works in their businesses today. It isn't just theory; the contributors to this book run different sized businesses on several continents, so there is undoubtedly something in this book for businesses of every size and stage of development.

Four Corners of the World

The following chapters cover a wide range of marketing topics. Because they have been written by people from the four corners of the world, each author uses the form of English in use where they live.

But English comes in many versions, with many spellings and grammatical constructions. As the editor of this book, I've not tried to standardise the English, but left it as written by the authors. This means you may see the same word spelt in several different ways depending on who wrote the chapter and the conventions in their part of the world.

We live in a very small world where we watch films and TV programmes made far from where we live. We read books, articles and blogs written by people who have English as their mother tongue or for whom it is their second, third, fourth or business language, so these English variations are unlikely to be a problem to most readers. I make a point of this only to avoid confusion and because your next customer could speak any one of hundreds of forms of English.

My advice is don't worry about the spellings and grammatical construction; instead, think about the content and how you can apply it to your business situation.

A Last Thought

There are literally thousands of ways to market any business. Each business is different and what works for one business may not work for the next.

So in this book you'll find authors saying that they think the best marketing strategy or tactic is x, y or z. In the next chapter you could find advice that countermands what you've just read.

This doesn't mean one is right and one is wrong. It means that you need to decide, with your new knowledge, what will work for your business. For example, some of my clients find video ads on Facebook work incredibly well for them, but for my business they are a total waste of time. The thing is we have different target audiences, with different products or services.

My advice is to read the chapters, decide what you think might work for you and then move forward slowly. For example, if you decide that Pay Per Click (PPC) ads might work for you then I'd suggest you spend some time on the websites of those people who have written about this or a related topic and learn more before spending a fortune. Investing a smallish sum in one of the products or services you'll find listed in the book will undoubtedly be a better first step than committing to a high-value contract that ties you in for ages.

If you want more information on any topic, use the links to the resources the authors have made available to you. Much of the further information they provide is free. However, you'll also see links to products and services that need to be paid for. Why? Simply because the authors are applying some of the marketing advice they are freely giving you.

So enjoy the book and learn what you can, but more importantly, follow up on what you learn. The most unsuccessful budding entrepreneurs I regularly meet are those who are going to get started tomorrow. The successful ones move faster and quickly implement what they learn.

Stefan Drew
Editor

CHAPTER 1

How To Market Any Business Without Spending Money

The Marketing Magician, Stefan Drew

The Big Marketing Myth

The biggest marketing myth ever perpetuated is that marketing is difficult, expensive and time-consuming.

Wrong.

Some of the best marketing strategies and tactics ever devised are either low cost or free, take little time and are very simple.

How do I know?

I've spent a lifetime in marketing. I started before the internet was invented, but I've also embraced digital marketing and now use a wide range of digital marketing techniques every day. Most of them are very low cost or even free. All of them are very effective.

That's not to say that the traditional methods of marketing no longer work. They do. In fact, if you integrate traditional and digital marketing you are on the road to mastering marketing.

There is another reason I know that there are simpler ways of achieving great marketing results. On a daily basis, I work with some of the leading marketing people in the world, many of whom have contributed chapters to this book. These people use simple marketing methods and many of these methods are free and take relatively little time.

Can Marketing Ever Be Free?

Yes.

People selling expensive marketing systems will argue with me and tell you there is no such thing as a free dinner - they would, wouldn't they? But there are thousands of marketing strategies, tactics and techniques that cost absolutely nothing to implement.

But let me define free. I consider any technique to be free if I don't pay money for it. So getting listed as an organic result on Page One of Google is free. You cannot pay to appear as an organic result on Page One of Google. So if you are on Page One of Google it can be a form of free marketing. Despite searches frequently returning millions of results, someone has to be on Page One of Google and it could be you if you produce a page that Google considers a good user experience. Everyone who has contributed to this book will be on Page One of Google for at least one search term. Many will appear for more than one. So could you.

Of course, if you want to pay for Search Engine Optimisation (SEO) services or for Pay Per Click (PPC) advertising, this will also get you on page one of Google. But though low cost, this isn't free. Despite not being free, it is still a very good marketing method and I recommend it. If you want to learn more, read Mike Seddon's chapter on Google Adwords.

You might also want to read Joey Bushnell's chapter on Facebook advertising. Both Facebook and Google

Adwords are excellent low cost ways to find prospects, but each takes a different approach.

Of course, appearing on Page One of Google means you need to understand SEO. Basic SEO is totally free and Eugene Farber's chapter will give you lots of clues. I also consider websites to be free!

At this stage I usually get people arguing with me, especially if they have spent a lot of money on a website (there are also ways to get free websites). But they miss the point. You can pay for website design and development (and it can be expensive), but once you have a website, adding extra pages is either low cost or totally free. There should be no additional charge. If you need to pay your developer to add new pages then you need to ask them to show you how, or if they say it is difficult you need to review your website and relationship with the developer. Modern website Content Management System (CMS) software is very simple to use. If you can type, cut and paste, you can produce a basic web page.

So let's recap. There are essentially two definitions of "Free Marketing". The first costs nothing at all, like getting on Page One of Google because you have great content and have paid attention to SEO basics.

My second definition of free is where you may have paid initially but additional usage is free. For example, once I've paid for my phone, taking photos and video is free.

Of course, the term "free" is largely about money and if you want to know more about money and your business, read Justin Krane's chapter.

More About Website Content

Many people have asked me why additional website content is important. They reason that once you've explained who you are and what you do your website is complete.

What they fail to understand is that our prospects and customers devour content. Whenever they have a question, want to make a purchase or have a spare moment, they are online searching. If you can work out what keeps them awake at night, and write great content about it, then there is a chance you will be able to write web content that people want, and that means it is likely to be indexed high up in Google's search index. It means that if you write good content and cover the SEO basics you are in the running to be indexed high up in the search results.

There are a few things you need to remember here. Getting on Page One is much easier than many people think, especially many web designers. The secret of good content is that you answer the question asked by the searcher. Let's assume you are an expert on gardening and write fantastic stuff about plants. You might write an article for a magazine about how the use of Latin plant names makes things like flower colour abundantly clear.

They might search for "How Latin plant names make colour abundantly clear".

Even though a search like this could return millions of pages, if you have a page that exactly deals with this specific question then you can beat all the pages that nearly, but not quite, answer that specific question.

Providing a good user experience is largely about answering the question asked and not a closely related question. Billions of questions are asked online every day so the secret of success in many ways has to be deciding on the questions your prospects will ask and answering them well. Doing this is free!

Why Do You Have A Website?

While I'm on websites, why do you bother with a website? It seems an obvious question but it is also one that few business people can answer. Read through the chapters in this book and I think you'll have a better idea when you've finished.

But let me give you some clues. It might be to help you make a profit for your business, but that doesn't mean you need to make the website about you and your business. Your website should be about your customer, their problem and how they can solve their problem (the fact that this might mean buying a product or service from you is almost coincidental!).

Another great free marketing tool associated with your website is Google Analytics. Knowing more about your customers will help you serve them more effectively.

Say you discover that you get a lot of traffic on your site from mobile devices. That's good, but say you know your website is not easily displayed on a phone or tablet. You could be losing loads of business. Google Analytics allows you to stop guessing about your website customers and to focus on reality.

If you also knew the age, gender and location of your buyers, as opposed to casual visitors who didn't buy, it would mean you could focus far more on targeting potential buyers. If you could also discover when genuine prospects and customers visit your site you might then decide to promote your website on social media or PPC at those specific times. Armed with information, you can significantly improve your profits.

Google Analytics provides huge volumes of traffic that large companies pay a fortune for. The standard version of Google Analytics is totally free and Vernon Riley unveils both its intricacies and simplicity in his chapter.

Time Is Money

People have often pointed out to me that time is money, so even free marketing is actually costing you money as it uses up valuable time.

This is true.

Time is money and marketing always takes time.

But so does everything else you do in your business. Manufacturing, buying, stocktaking, selling - everything takes time and therefore costs money.

My advice is to look at this from another angle.

Ask yourself if your use of time is cost-effective? Are you getting a good Return on Investment (ROI)?

In other words, if you spend a single unit of currency, how much will you get back? In most cases, if we spend one unit we want to get more than one unit back. Ideally we want 10 or 20 units back.

So think about your time in terms of your investment in time rather than deciding that "free" is bad. All marketing takes time and we need to balance actual spend plus time against our income from that investment.

The internet has made outsourcing much easier so you might decide that some free marketing techniques could be profitably outsourced. You will of course have to pay someone for the work but the techniques used can still be free.

An Effective Marketing Strategy

Trying to run a business without a strategy and plan to guide you isn't a great idea.

Say you wanted to travel to somewhere 1,000 miles away. You'd get a map, some timetables, sort out the costs and decide if you will be travelling by air, road or rail.

In other words, you'd plan. You'd also devise a strategy like not travelling in the rainy season.

This is all common sense stuff.

So why do so many businesses fail to plan. Lots of them, and I include some huge businesses, plan badly or not at all. Some have failed because of it. They haven't considered how things like new technologies will affect them. For example, some photographic film manufacturers didn't think ahead and plan for a changing future. The result was that digital photography finished them.

Other businesses didn't plan for a wet summer, which is really bad if all you do is rent out beach chairs. Good planning overcomes these problems.

This book will provide you with a whole range of things you can add to your marketing plan. But before you go that far, how about you decide on your strategy? To help you with that it would also be a good idea to read Peter Sandeen's chapter about how marketing really works and Donnie Bryant's chapter on good news.

Planning Your Strategy

Some of the companies I've been approached by had business and marketing strategies that weighed several kilos. No one ever referred to them and they were a waste of time.

A good strategy achieves something very simple: it explains how you are going to get from A to B. In our travel example above, the strategy could be to use a mix of air and rail travel and only travel in summer.

The best strategies, like the ones above, take just a few lines.

Every business strategy will vary a bit as we are all trying to achieve different things. But taking a high-level perspective usually makes things much simpler.
For example, my guess is you don't want to spend too much money on marketing and want to save time. So here are my first two lines of your marketing strategy:

Reduce marketing costs.
Automate marketing wherever possible.

My guess is that you don't want to leave things to chance either.

As John Wanamaker said, "Half the money I spend on advertising is wasted, the trouble is I don't know which half".

The way to ensure this never applies to you is simple:

Test, measure and improve your marketing.

Common sense tells me that if we test several ways to do things and measure our marketing responses (not just our advertising) then we can stop anything that doesn't work and this will improve our marketing.

At first glance this might seem time-consuming and expensive, but it isn't.

For instance, say you decide to send a free email to your customers and want to optimise your results. Well one thing that affects this is the subject line. The question is, which one will work? You'll know if you test it.

Send 10% of your list one subject line and 10% of your list another subject line and measure which one gets the best response.

Now send the remaining 80% an email with the most responsive subject line. This doesn't take long and is an example of free marketing. If one subject line provides a 10, 20 or 50% improvement in sales, the ROI on the time you spent on this is going to be very high. Even if it is only 1-2% it can still be worthwhile when aggregated with other improvements.

Another example would be PPC advertising.

Set up two to three ads that vary in just one small way. Maybe it's the header line or call to action. Test them for a while and then look at the PPC stats. This takes very little time but in my experience can increase response rates by up to 1,000%.

Do Prospects Ignore You?

No one ever deliberately designed an advert or website for people to ignore. We want people to react to them. We want prospects to phone us, email us, subscribe to us, sponsor us, buy from us - we want them to engage with us.
So my next strategic element is:

Engage more effectively.

Let me give you an example here.

I recently spoke to the CEO of a business with a turnover of £20m. He complained that marketing didn't work for them.

So I asked what they did to market the business and was given a comprehensive list of activities that had recently included building a new website. Then I asked what the purpose of the website was. He told me it was to showcase their offer so people would phone them for an appointment. But apparently since spending a lot of money on the new website, things had got worse and they weren't getting many calls.

Then I asked him to behave like a new visitor and go to the website. He did and found an item he "wanted" and I asked him to phone for an appointment. He immediately started to dial an internal number and I stopped him. I asked him how he knew what the number was and of course he said he knew it because he employed the people in that department.

I reminded him that he was meant to be behaving like a new website visitor and I wanted him to find the number on the website.

After several minutes, he had to admit defeat. The number wasn't on the website. No phone numbers were on the website! That's why calls had dropped so dramatically.

The problem is that this type of situation is not uncommon. I know people in dozens of countries that have made similar mistakes.

We need to engage with people at all levels, from providing them with telephone numbers to talking to prospects and customers.

An Easy Life

Few people ever tell me they want a complex life. Most want an easy life.

And yet many people devise incredibly complex marketing systems. Prospects are bounced from A to B to C to D to E to F and so it goes on. At each point there are opportunities to get it wrong, for the prospect to walk away and for the whole process to collapse.

In a really simple world if you wanted a drink, I'd hold out a glass of water and you'd buy it. It is a simple model. But in many businesses there are too many steps in the process and it costs them sales.

So my final line of strategy is:

Simplify all marketing.

RATES Marketing

So there you have it, a basic marketing strategy in five lines:

Reduce marketing costs
Automate marketing wherever possible
Test, measure and improve your marketing
Engage more effectively
Simplify all marketing

Your business is unlike any other but in my experience few businesses would go astray if they used the **RATES Marketing Strategy** as a basis for their own strategy.

Finally on this topic there is an essential we should all remember: people prefer to do business with people they know, like, trust and respect. We all need to think about this and build it into our business and marketing strategies. It needs to become an integral element of our mindset. Wally Waldron writes about trust and gaining lifelong buyers in his chapter.

More Traditional "Free" Marketing Ideas

Marketing didn't start with the digital age. It was flourishing long before.

It wasn't so different from today with lots of businesses wanting to take your money for things they tried to persuade you that you couldn't do yourself. So they used smoke and mirrors to make it look difficult and told you anything free had to be bad. According to these people, if it didn't cost a lot it was worthless and so were you. Well value, cost and worth don't always equate. Michael Zipursky explains more in his chapter about values.

But even before the digital age, the smart people could still find low-cost and free marketing. We all knew advertising in newspapers was "trending" and we had ad sales people phoning to sell us ad space all the time (it used to amuse me that they phoned rather than relied on their own advertising).

We knew papers still had lots of readers, but that ads were expensive and it wasn't easy to measure them. Sales reps nearly always started by telling us which competitors were advertising with them and tried to use this to pressure us into advertising.

But whereas the public understood that ads were a form of sales letter, and perhaps not totally honest, they also believed that most of what was written in articles was more objective. Some of us therefore realised that if we wrote press releases and sent them to the paper, our news would appear in articles and be believed.

A press release with the Who, What, How, Why, When and Where of a news story was something we could easily produce and quickly send to a newsroom. Do it and there was a good chance that we'd be in line for free newspaper coverage.

Today we call them media releases. Media releases can be a very quick way to get news out. In my experience, it can take as little as 20 minutes to get a story online via a media release. This is almost as fast as social media, or a blog, so is really worth considering. And, of course, it is totally free.

Meny Hoffman's chapter on brand values and traditional marketing techniques may well have you wondering if you ever need to go digital again.

Berlin Wall

If you delve back in history, or if you are as old as me, you'll know about the fall of the Berlin Wall. This was a momentous period at the end of the Cold War. It happened in November 1989 and was covered by every national media outlet around the world.
As luck had it, I was in Berlin the night the Wall came down. The following morning I phoned my local radio station, back in the UK, and explained where I was. The result was that I was live on air within minutes. This situation didn't need a media release. A simple phone call was all that was needed.

What the local media in the UK wanted was a local angle, and I was able to provide it live "as their man in Berlin". In the weeks that followed, I was in the studios many times talking about something where my only real level of expertise was the fact I'd been there.

Today, my business and marketing stories are on major websites and in leading papers and magazines across my own country and many others. Because the media companies now recognise my expertise, they often phone me to comment on breaking news. It gets me on the BBC and other major media outlets at least once a month.

This isn't unique to me. Other contributors to this book do similar things. You can do this in your business. It isn't hard, and once again, it's free.

As I pointed out above, you don't always need to be the most knowledgeable person on a subject to get on air.

Having said that, I'm sure that you have expertise in quite a few key areas. Without your expertise, you wouldn't be where you are today; however, most of us don't recognise our own knowledge. We think lots of people know as much as us. That might be so, but the only person who will get in the media is the one who holds their hand up and is seen by the media!

A twist on the Berlin story is to look for trending stories online, write a post and bounce people over to it via social media. If what you write contributes to the original story by pointing out a new angle, it could trend on the back of the original story. The other real plus here is that journalists are looking for an angle and if they like yours, they will now chase you for an interview. In his chapter in this book, Professor Srikumar Rao writes about getting people to chase you. My technique is just one of the many variations he suggests.

There's another twist on media releases: write an article or column for a website, blog, magazine or newspaper instead. This takes you beyond being an expert and establishes you as an authority. You might think you can't write a series of articles but I bet you can list the 5 to 10 most frequent questions people ask you. So, make the list of FAQs and then answer them. If it makes it easier, sit with a friend who can ask the questions so you can naturally give them an answer. This makes your answers far less formal and probably much easier to understand. If you use your mobile phone or laptop to record the answers, you can then write them up
afterwards. And if writing isn't your thing, then employ someone to do that for you. Even the best experts use "ghostwriters" and it can be much lower cost than you might imagine when you shop around online.

Talk To People

Sometimes we get so bogged down with highly technical marketing processes that we forget the basics.

When did you last phone a customer or prospect? There are some things we can do remotely but there's nothing like personal contact to cement a relationship. And the best of it is that a quick phone call can be free. For more on business relationships read John Corcoran's chapter.

Skype is my favourite free phone service but don't forget all the minutes you get with your mobile, so many of which never get used.

Of course, some people find making a "cold" call very difficult. But these aren't cold calls. These are calls to people you know. These people are already warm leads.

Even then some people aren't sure what to say. I tend to start off with a follow-up call after a customer has placed an order so that I can simply thank them for their order. This is so uncommon that customers are surprised by it.

Or if the person is a prospect, I might call to invite them to an event; calling is so much more personal than email. Or maybe I'll call and ask them for some advice. People love it when you recognise their expertise.

The main thing is to build a relationship. That said, you wouldn't phone someone to thank them for ordering a small item because it would be too time-consuming.

But what if they have bought an item for which they pay a small amount every month. Ian Brodie contacts everyone who buys his monthly Momentum Club membership, but he uses a slight twist to the phone idea. He sends them a personalised video. When I got mine it blew me away. Ian's contributed a chapter to this book on marketing's missing link. It's worth a read.

Another chapter worth reading is Jonathan Altfeld's piece on using NLP to get highly qualified leads.

Public Relations

PR is all about your reputation. It is free unless you engage a PR agency. PR is essentially about what people say about you when you are not in the room. The things that impact it most are the way you do business, things like great customer service and going that extra mile for the customer.

PR agencies can spend your money on eye-catching gimmicks that get people talking but they aren't in front of customers 24/7. Great PR begins in your car park, it continues in your spotlessly clean toilets and continues whenever you think customer first. In the UK, companies like John Lewis focus on the customer and their reputation is great. They have recognised that happy customers spend more and keep coming back and that means they make profit when others go bust.

Other companies focus on costs and profits, or pile it high and sell it cheap. Lots of the names that were really good at this are no longer in business.

PR is about your attitude to your customers and as a marketing technique can cost nothing.

Referrals

So many people tell me that they get most of their business by word of mouth or referrals that it must be a great marketing strategy. But when I ask them how they use referrals strategically, what their plan is, they look confused. The problem is they don't have a referrals strategy. Steve Gordon has contributed a great chapter on referral strategies. I've tried Steve's strategies - they really work and cost next to nothing to implement.

Live Events

If talking to people is such a great marketing tactic, and I'm convinced it is, then attending or running live events starts to make sense.

For many people, a live event will be something like a webinar, a networking event or an exhibition.
Networking can be really effective but it depends entirely on attending events where you'll find your ideal prospect. Those selling networking will also tell you it is as much about who the people you meet can introduce you to. I'm not going to say they have it wrong, but that is a bit like saying that it isn't who reads your newspaper advert but who they can introduce you to.

Having said that, if you select the right type of event at which to network (note I didn't say networking event) then networking can be very effective. For example, the CEOs in one of my niche sectors are notorious for not socialising and networking, but once a year every single one of them spends a few days at a week-long national conference. If you want to meet them then you have to go to this event. It isn't called a networking event but it is where this niche networks.

The other type of event I personally favour is what I'll call an information event. It works like this. You decide on the niche you want to network with, let's say it is small businesses in your town. You decide on a topic that keeps those small businesses awake at night and run a short information event on it.

In my case, I know lots of small businesses struggle with marketing so I've run an evening event where my colleagues and I invite the businesses to come and hear about how to market a small business without spending money. The session takes place at the end of the working day, I do a 45-minute presentation with 15 minutes for questions and answers, and we don't try to sell anything to them. What we do get is a list of attendees and in the follow-up email, where we thank them for attending, we make a small offer that might be of interest.

My claim to fame with these events is that we market them without a marketing budget and we normally get around 200 attendees. It is one of the best demonstrations of free marketing I know.

Tom Zeeb has his own take on running live events and has written a chapter on it.

Free Digital Marketing Strategies

I've already mentioned that websites can be effectively free and that you can measure all sorts of stats via Google Analytics. But there is more to it than that.

Let's go right back to basics. No marketing strategy, plan or technique will succeed unless you have one essential. I don't care if it is a website, PR campaign or whatever.

You need clarity about your purpose and that of your business.

There's an old saying: when you are fighting crocodiles, it is hard to remember that the purpose of the exercise was to drain the swamp.

That assumes you once knew you were there to drain the swamp. Of all the reasons for marketing not working, having no clarity of purpose has to be number one. Laura and Dominic Ashley-Timms have written a great chapter on clarity and a few other essentials that will have an impact on your traditional and digital marketing approaches.

But let me get back to websites. Say you get 1,000 visitors a day or month on your website. Would getting 2,000 visitors to the site be the most cost-effective way to double your profit?
It would probably cost you twice as much effort or money on an ongoing basis. But what if you tried a different approach.

Say you spent just a couple of hours on a one-off exercise and improved the conversion rate of your landing pages? Say you increased sales by a factor of two, three or even four? Wouldn't that be far more cost-effective? And if all you needed to do was redesign the page, change the colours of a few buttons or change a word or two in a headline, would that be as good as free marketing? Sometimes it is that simple.

Bnonn Tennant explains about improving landing pages in his chapter.

In another chapter, Nick Jervis looks at how to get more enquiries from your website. Nothing that Nick or Bnonn explains is very complex and none of their ideas cost much money.

Social Media

Social media is one of those topics we are all told we must be doing if we are to succeed in our business. There is something that most people miss though.

Social media is just a tool in much the same way as a billboard or a leaflet is a tool. It isn't the tool that is important; rather, the message we use the tool to convey is what is important.

The least important types of message are those that tell others what you had for breakfast, by which I mean you need to say something that is meaningful to your business audience. Your message has to say something of value to them that will engage with them, something that they can comment on, maybe like, or better still follow a call to action that moves them along your sales funnel. This might be to download an information product, ask a question, answer a survey or a thousand other things.

Virtually every form of social media allows some of the above. However, what confuses many social media users is which ones are appropriate to their business. There is only one right answer to this. You have to decide what it is you want to achieve and find the social media route that helps you achieve your objectives. Clearly the social media platform you select must be visited by your prospective audience in sufficient volume to make economic sense. It might be that more than one satisfies this criteria and you then need to decide if you want to focus on one or more platforms at once. My advice is normally to choose the one you feel most comfortable with and perfect that one before attempting a second or third platform.

Although likes and follows can be important, what really counts is meeting our ultimate objective. I know some people say a thousand likes on Facebook will convert to a small but predictable sales stream, but personally I'd rather see a simpler process.

For example, at the time of writing I'm working with a lot of colleges that wish to target school leavers with details of their apprenticeships, college courses and degree-level offers. Despite media stories to the contrary, in the UK at present, Facebook is still the place to reach these young people. In most cases, my chosen method is to use animated video advertising that bounces the viewers to an external website. The overall costs are extremely low and ROI very, very high. To put figures to it, video ad views are currently (October 2014) costing me between £0.06 and £0.10 a view, with the value of a "sale" being anything up to £10k.

Another advantage of this type of advertising is that we are able to segment our audience by location, age, gender and interests at no additional cost.

Facebook is seen by many as only being suitable for promoting products or services to young people; however, nothing could be further from the truth. Facebook is full of adults as well and is one of those free marketing platforms I use daily to help my clients engage with older audiences.

In my case, I advertise winemaking degrees on Facebook. Another perfect example of using Facebook to promote to adults is the way some businesses use Facebook groups as a question and answer forum for their customers. These groups can be "closed" (accessible to members) or open to anyone, and are a brilliant free marketing resource for any business.

LinkedIn

Another social media platform I use every day is LinkedIn. It is probably the most extensive and up-to-date business database ever created.

Not only do you have a search facility that enables you to find virtually every type of niche operator in the world, but you can also find people very similar to them at the click of a button and at no cost.

Once again there is an extensive network of business groups (far superior to Facebook in my opinion) and of course targeted advertising (expensive in my experience).

Like Facebook, LinkedIn is free to use, unless you decide to take a premium level of membership, which I've never found necessary except as a test.

Across the world there are thousands of social media platforms from which to choose and most have a level of free membership.

And once you've made contact with new prospects, sooner or later you'll need to have a sales conversation with them. Matthew Kimberley is the expert I listen to in this area and I recommend his chapter on sales conversations.

Video

We are visual animals. We are stimulated by movement and respond to it. So it is hardly surprising that YouTube is now the second largest search engine in the world.

The great thing is that video is probably the most powerful marketing technique we can employ and it is largely free. It is possible to pay companies large sums to make professional videos to promote our businesses but most of us now own a video camera, sometimes without even realising it. Most mobile phones contain a good-quality video camera, and apps are also available for phones that will edit and post video straight to YouTube at no cost whatsoever.

The world of video is changing rapidly. We can now use mobiles to film 8mm sequences, apply other special effects, edit and add soundtracks. Video can be conventional film, animated, stop frame or use hundreds of other techniques. It is changing so quickly that, rather than write more, I'm going to send you to a micro site that contains a video series on How to make videos at no cost.

About Stefan Drew

Stefan Drew is introduced by the BBC and other leading media companies as The Marketing Magician. The name was first coined by one of his clients and seemed to sum up what he did so much that he trademarked it.

Stefan's career in marketing commenced before the advent of digital marketing, which meant he mastered marketing basics long before he became an authority on digital marketing. Believing that many people were being ripped off by self-proclaimed "experts" selling expensive "snake oil" marketing remedies, his strategy has been to focus on "free" marketing, which has been proven to provide a good return on investment.

As part of this strategy, he provides free advice to his two niche markets via **StefanDrew.com** and **ProviderMasterMind.com.**

Stefan's strategy is based on the fact that if you provide value in advance, customers will offer contracts once ready to buy. Although this strategy seems "too good to be true", it has seen Stefan make a good living over a lifetime in marketing.

Subscribe to his regular free newsletter at **StefanDrew.com** to learn more about how his strategy could work for you.

LinkedIn http://uk.linkedin.com/in/stefandrew

Twitter @stefandrewe

Google + Personal Profile
google.com/+StefanDrewMarketingMagician

CHAPTER 2

How To Communicate Value And Make More Money

Michael Zipursky

Anton runs a successful management consulting company. His clients include Boeing, Cognizant, Raytheon, GE and others. During a three-week period, Anton did a few things he'd never done before, and he brought in an extra $1Million for his company.

Sam sells online courses and guides for small business owners. With one simple change his sales increased 43% and they continue to grow month-over-month.

Barb is an author and speaker in the healthcare industry. She also implemented a new business strategy that allowed her to charge 700% more than before while turning a small project into a 12-month payday.

These three entrepreneurs have completely different businesses and business models. Yet they all succeeded in growing their revenues and profits quickly and sustainably.

In this chapter, I'm going to share the best and fastest way to grow your business and revenue. You'll learn the same strategies and approaches that Anton, Sam, Barb and countless others I've coached and consulted with have used to achieve phenomenal business results. You'll also learn how to apply these powerful practices to reach your personal and professional goals.

The fastest way to grow your business is to increase your prices. This is hands down the most direct and effective way to grow your revenues.

To increase your prices and make more money than ever before, your focus must be on providing value.

And the more value you deliver, the more you can charge.

Once you adopt this approach, your revenue and income can skyrocket. Many of my clients have doubled and even tripled their revenues in months, not years as a direct result of increasing their prices.

Tip #1-It's Not About YOU

Okay, we've established that to charge more you need to provide greater value. So how do you do that?
First, you need to learn how to demonstrate and communicate the value you are delivering. The most successful business owners do so by following the approach below:

1. They start by listening. To successfully communicate the value you deliver, you'll need to discover your buyers' biggest problems and the desired results they hope to achieve in choosing your product or service.

2. They ask the right questions. To learn exactly what your buyer cares about most, you should ask as many questions as you can to discover the business impact caused by the problem they are experiencing. Use these questions to guide the conversation, and you will receive valuable information that helps you better communicate the value you are delivering. For example:

- What is the main area you'd like to improve in your business/life?
- What is its current impact on your business/life?
- How long have you been dealing with it?
- Why have you decided to deal with it now?
-Tell me more about your current situation (income/weight/health/happiness/morale, etc.) and how you'd like it to change?
- What are the greatest challenges holding you back from achieving your goals?
- What is the value of one new project to your business, and how much will dealing with this problem help you achieve stronger business growth?

3. They determine *real value*. Once you've asked lots of good questions and have plenty of information, you'll be able to determine the *real value* of your offering to the buyer. If your buyer wants to attract more clients, and one new client is worth $35,000, that's critical information to know, and I'll show you how to use it shortly.

4. They understand the cost of standing still. When it comes to communicating the value you provide to clients, it's easy to overlook the cost of staying where they are. In your buyer's case, not only do they stand to gain from the benefits they'll receive from buying your

product or service; they're also losing money every day, week, and month that they don't change their situation and solve the problem they have. If your buyer wants better health, every day they don't improve their health increases their risk of additional health problems. If they want to attract more clients and increase their revenue, every day they don't take action constitutes lost revenue for them. If they are currently earning $20k a month and want to increase that to $50k a month, they are losing the difference with each and every month that goes by without action.

5. They think and speak in terms of value, not cost. As you begin to understand the true value you are providing, make sure it's in line with your pricing; i.e. if your product or service will save your buyer $12k (the value), you'll have a hard time selling your solution for $41k.

On the other hand, if your offering produces $250k in value for your buyer, charging $41k is right on the mark. Later, I'll share how to set your pricing to ensure the right pricing-to-return-on-investment ratio for buyers.

Tip #2-Buyers Like Options (And So Will You)

A sure fire way to increase your revenue is to package up your offerings and provide options for your buyers.

Imagine hiring an architect to help you design your house. You spend time explaining how important natural light is, and how much you'd like to have a covered area for your kids to play in during the winter. The architect takes this information and provides you with a proposal. "Here it is," she says. "This is what I'd recommend, and the cost will be $80,000."

If that's the budget you had in mind, and if the recommendation is exactly what you want, then all is good. However, what if the architect's proposal doesn't capture everything you had in mind - either because your budget is different or because you want something different?

Whether you're offering a service like this architect or selling a product, failing to provide your buyers with options will vastly limit the growth potential of your business.

In this case, the architect would have been much better off providing two or three options. When you offer only one option to your buyer, you're basically saying, whether you mean to or not, "take it or leave it."

By providing options for your buyer, you will significantly increase the chance of them saying "Yes" to one of them.

No longer is the conversation centered around "Buy this because it's your only choice." It becomes, "which option would be best for you?" That's a simple yet powerful difference. And I'm going to show you how to make a lot more money from it.

Profiting From Choice

Most businesses find that offering three options is most effective. Here's how to lay out your buyer's options:

Option 1 - This is their lowest price option. It includes the minimum service offering or features your buyer needs to reach a successful outcome. It offers value for the investment.

Option 2 - This option includes the services or features from Option 1, plus additional services, features or products that provide even more value to your buyer. If Option 1 is a book, Option 2 could be a book plus DVD. Or, if you're offering a workshop in Option 1,

Option 2 might include a workshop and coaching for three months. The key is to offer so much additional value that a buyer considering Option 1 is pulled to Option 2.

Option 3 - This is the option with the greatest value and highest price point. When I work through this process with my consulting clients, I always recommend that they start with a blank canvas. I tell them to imagine that their buyer has plenty of resources and that money isn't an issue - as if their buyer has said, "I have money to invest, so what can you offer me that will help me solve the problem I have or reach the result I'm after in the shortest time possible?" Option 3 usually includes everything from Option 2, plus additional services, features or products.

If Option 1 is priced at $1,000, Option 2 may be $1,600 and Option 3 would be offered at $3,000.

You'll notice that Option 3 represents a significant jump in price. The reason for this comes down to how buyers make decisions and the percentage of people that will choose each option. The research of two psychologists, Tversky and Kahneman, indicates the following:

Option 1 provides an entry point to working with you. It's for buyers that have limited resources or don't fully trust their relationship with you. It allows them to see what it's like to buy from you, and they often go on to buy more down the road. Typically, 15% of buyers will go with Option 1.

Option 2 will be the most popular. When making a buying decision, most people don't want to be seen as choosing the least expensive option. They want value, but they can't justify going with the most expensive option. This lands them right in the middle, and you'll find that roughly 70-80% of buyers will choose Option 2 as a result.
Your third option isn't for everyone, and that's fine. It's for the buyer that wants the best and is aggressively seeking results. They don't see the price as a cost, but rather as an investment. And they are willing to pay for it. These buyers will typically represent 5% of the total.

Tversky and Kahneman also identified another factor at play in purchase decision-making, and it's called Anchoring. What it means is that, when people hear or see a larger number, they will typically perceive a lower number they hear or see right after the first to be significantly less than if they had only seen the lower number.

In the context of pricing, this is significant. If your product sells for $1,000 and that's your only offer, that's what your buyer will judge. However, if you also have a $3,000 offer, when the buyer sees your second option for $1,600 and your third for $1,000, both will seem very reasonable in comparison. The $1,000 and $1,600 options haven't changed - but they've been anchored by a higher priced option, which makes them *seem* significantly lower than if they sat by themselves.

When I take my clients through this process, what I see time and again is that most sellers focus on Option 1. By providing two additional options to buyers, almost immediately your revenue will increase. Just as importantly, your buyers will be happier with the enhanced value you deliver.

The Case For ROI: It's Not About You- Part Two

An extremely effective way to communicate value to buyers is to demonstrate that your product or service will produce a significant return on investment for them.

When your buyer is confident that every dollar they invest with you will return a greater value than that dollar, any hesitation to purchase from you fades away.

So how do you position your offering to provide the greatest return on investment possible?

Similar to asking the right questions to uncover the real problems and challenges driving your buyer to take action now, positioning return on investment starts by asking strategic questions.

The answers to these questions allow you to price your offerings in a way that provides your buyer with value and a positive return on investment, while maximizing your compensation.

In a few moments, I'll share the formula you can use to set your pricing. Before that, let's review the type of results-focused questions you'll need to ask to gather the information required to use the formula:

- What will these results mean for your bottom line?
- How will these results impact your company?
- What will this mean to you personally?
- What will a positive return on investment look like for you?
- What will your anticipated savings (or increased profit) be over the next two to five years?
- How will this benefit your customers and vendors, or provide you with an edge over your competition?

- What will happen if you don't move forward (and invest in or get help with ______)?

Another line of questioning which is critically important revolves around intangibles.

These are the benefits and results your buyer will receive from buying from you, but which can't be quantified as easily as an increase in sales or a decrease in costs. This doesn't diminish their importance.

When it comes to selling the intangibles include:

- Safety: how much safer will the buyer be as a result of your product or service?
- Comfort: how much more comfortable will the buyer be than they are currently?
- Peace of Mind: how much worry or stress will your product or service remove from the buyer's life?
- Ego: how much more confident and/or better off will your buyer feel after investing in your offering?

While it's difficult to assign a specific numeric value to each of these intangibles, they each impact a buyer's decision.

Getting answers to these questions should be straightforward, if you're selling a service as you have the opportunity to meet or talk on the phone with your ideal buyers.

However, even businesses selling products have ample opportunity to ask these valuable questions. You can approach your current or past buyers for feedback, call up a group of prospective buyers, or possibly conduct an online survey. You can even use an online advertising platform like Google Adwords to drive targeted traffic to a questionnaire designed to shed light on the true value connected to the intangible benefits your product or services provide.

Because asking these questions will provide you with insight into the *real value* your buyers will receive in working with you, failure to ask these questions likely means you're leaving money on the table during each and every sale you make.

The ROI Formula

Once you've received numerous like-minded answers, you'll be ready to use the ROI Formula:

ROI + Annual + Intangible = Pricing

This formula is part science and part art.

Here's how to break it down:

- ROI: Add up all the quantifiable value your offering provides. If you're helping people to reduce their operating costs and improve their profit margin by 5%, and that leads to an additional $500,000 in revenue this year, use that number.

- Annual: Will your buyer be able to continue receiving the benefits your product or service will provide for more than a year? If yes, be sure to multiply by this factor. Continuing with our previous example, if the $500,000 increase will last for at least two years, the value you're creating is at least $1M. I typically suggest that my clients assume a factor of two or three years because, even if the buyer will realize value for a longer period of time, many factors can come up that impact their results.

Intangibles: While you can't assign a dollar value to these, you can and should include them in the formula. You will certainly use them in your sales conversations and proposals because they influence buyers' decisions.

3-10X ROI

A great ROI ratio to aim for is to produce a three to 10 times return for your buyer.

In this case, if your buyer will receive $1.2M in value, you could charge as little as $120,000 to provide them with a 10X return. You could also go as high as $400,000 to provide a 3X return.

Using this formula, and basing your pricing on value, ensures that your client will be thrilled and that you will receive significant compensation for the value you create.

I always aim to provide my clients with a 6X to 10X return, and many see much better results. Whatever scale of return you decide on, ensure that your clients always see significant value and upside in buying from you.

Finally...Embrace The Flow

Product Flow

If you're selling a product and you don't have other products to sell to your buyers after the first sale, you're leaving a great deal of money on the table.

There are many ways you can add compelling products to your business.

For example:

- Create a product that customers pay for monthly. Examples of this include supplements and membership-based offerings.

- Have a higher-priced product that your customers can buy after they've made their first purchase.

- Offer services to support and add value to your customers' initial purchases. This could include consulting and coaching, or ongoing maintenance and training.

Service Flow

If you're selling services, the sooner you switch to a value-based sales model the faster you'll increase your revenue and profitability. The biggest mistake service-focused businesses make is charging by the hour.
Hourly rates aren't based on value, and they severely limit your income potential. To significantly grow your revenues, you'll be faced with hiring an ever-growing number of staff or increasing your hourly fees to levels that scare off most buyers.

In addition, when you charge by the hour your interests and those of your buyers are not aligned. Your buyers will likely avoid contacting you as much as possible when they know that the more they call, the more they'll pay. You'll also find that you're constantly trying to do more so you can earn more.

By using a value-based selling approach, service-oriented businesses can focus on the value and return on investment they provide to their clients rather than the work they do for their clients.

Imagine that...less work for more money!

As I Was Saying...

To skyrocket your revenues, ask lots of strategic questions and learn how you can help your buyers solve their problems and overcome their challenges. Then give them three options, use pricing based on value, and always be thinking about what other products or services you could provide to add value beyond the initial sale. What else do your buyers need your help with? How can you provide them with even more support?

Consider what you can offer that would provide your clients with the highest level of value and the greatest return on investment. This may take the form of additional consulting, coaching, training, speaking, workshops, or done-for-you services.

As you put these strategies into action, you'll be able to communicate value more effectively, increase your price-points and earn significantly more than you ever have before.

About Michael Zipursky

Michael Zipursky, CEO of Consulting Success, is an expert in helping consultants and coaches create marketing systems that consistently attract their ideal clients and significantly increase their income and fees. Michael's coaching clients regularly experience a 200-300% increase in revenue within 8-12 weeks. His corporate clients include Panasonic, Dow Jones, Financial Times, and the Royal Bank among others in over 23 industries around the world. Michael's work has been featured in numerous publications, including Marketing Profs, Huffington Post, Maclean's, KISS Metrics, HR Executive, Consultant News, and Professional Marketer. Over 5000 consultants have participated in Michael's trainings and over 22,000 read his weekly newsletter.

If you'd like to learn how to consistently attract your ideal clients, increase your fees and grow your business, request Michael's FREE Marketing Roadmap Session. This is a complimentary strategic session where Michael will show you step-by-step how to get more clients, earn more from every project and grow your business without overwhelm. Schedule your call with Michael here: **http://www.consultingsuccess.com/jvbook**

CHAPTER 3

How Marketing Works - Honestly

Peter Sandeen

If you aren't perfectly clear about what your marketing is supposed to do, you'll struggle with it. That might seem obvious, but it's not enough to say that your goal is to "increase sales" or "reach as many people as possible."

To reach your business goals, you need to understand what makes marketing effective. So let's start by looking at how marketing really works.

Marketing should persuade people to view your products or services as highly desirable and point out compelling reasons to buy them.

Therefore, your marketing should focus on communicating the reasons people should consider your products or services and *offer compelling reasons to buy them.* ***The more compelling the reasons, the more people are persuaded. The more people are persuaded, the more sales you make from your marketing efforts.***

However, you can't persuade everyone; you have to focus on persuading specific groups of people, that is, your target customers.

The most persuasive, compelling reasons for your target customers to pay attention to you and your products or services–and buy them–form your value proposition.

In other words, your marketing should make people understand your value proposition.

When it does, it's as effective as it can be.

More on your value proposition in a moment, but that's how marketing should work.

Maybe such a brief explanation seems overly simplistic. But it isn't. Getting people to notice you and your products and buy them is all that marketing is supposed to do.

That said, figuring out the most persuasive reasons for your target customers to buy your products or services means crafting your value proposition carefully. And that's *not* so simple.

Even evaluating your ideas about *potential* persuasive reasons can be difficult. That's because we're so close to our own ideas (and emotionally involved) that seeing them objectively is challenging.

We'll consider the key aspects of persuasive reasons to take action and buy. But first, let's look at target customers and why you absolutely need to know yours to succeed in business.

Choose Your Target Customers Wisely

A persuasive reason to act for one person can be totally irrelevant to another, and that's why you can't expect everyone to buy what you sell.

If you target everyone, you attract no one.

Let's say your product is the best option for one person, but for another person it's only mediocre.

If you modify your product or marketing angle to make it a great choice for the second person, you're probably making so many compromises that the first person no longer wants to buy it.

Before you can consider what will persuade someone to buy, you need to be clear about the kind of people you want to persuade.

Developing a clear target customer takes some effort; several questions and details must be considered. But here are the two most revealing questions:

1. What are the most frustrating problems your prospective customers struggle with that your product or service can solve?

2. What are the most important goals they struggle to reach that your product or service will help with?

The answers–if they're detailed and specific enough–describe your target customers. If the answers don't accurately describe someone, that person isn't your target customer.

Now remember, if you list a large number of qualities, very few people will fit the description. Finding the right balance of specific-enough but not-too-specific descriptions can take some trial and error.

Start by imagining your ideal customer. What sort of person has the kinds of problems you can solve? The kinds of goals you can help them reach with your product or service?

The description might end up being too general or too specific, but it's a good start. You can then add details or remove the least important details to make the description fit a smaller or larger group of people.

Focus On The Benefits, Not The Features

When you've identified your target customer, you can consider what makes you and your products and services valuable to them.

What benefits do you offer?

Forget features, focus on benefits.

A benefit describes an outcome that your target customers perceive as a positive result of purchasing your product or services–it's not something that creates or enables the result. In other words, your product features aren't nearly as important in marketing as the practical benefits those features lead to.

For example, the strength of eyeglass lenses are a *feature*, which has no value of its own. However, what the *feature* results in (seeing clearly) is a *benefit*.

Note that "first level benefits" aren't necessarily seen as benefits. You have to dig deep enough to find the benefits that your target customers *perceive* as meaningful benefits. Something that goes a bit deeper into their needs and wants, even deep down to basic psychological needs.

For example, a longer sailboat is faster and has more indoor space–these are first level benefits. Some people might think additional speed and space are benefits in themselves, but they're just features.

The actual benefits are that you get to your destination before evening, you can make longer trips, and you have enough space to prepare food and sleep comfortably.

Feeling proud of a fast sailboat is also a benefit that goes a bit deeper, and a desire to fit in, belong, or be admired and respected goes deeper still. But the fact that it's fast is simply a fact–a feature.

What you personally think about your products, services, and marketing is almost irrelevant. All that matters is how your target customers perceive them.

In most cases, you know your products and services better than your customers. And therefore you can appreciate the finer details more than your customers can.

So be careful. Unless you're just like your target customers, they're likely to see and value different benefits than you.

Even though it's difficult, you have to forget what you think about your products and services. Instead, focus on how your target customers see them; they're the people you're trying to persuade, not yourself.

Finding the benefits that matter the most to your target customers can be tricky. But here's a simple exercise that will get you started:

1. List all of your product's features.

2. List all the benefits each of the features can provide.

3. Consider which of the benefits are the most important to your target customers.

Even the most mundane products (and services) have plenty of features. And all of those features have some practical benefits.

For example, here's a partial list of a basic yellow pencil's features:

1. It's yellow.
2. It's a #2.
3. It's round.
4. It's wooden.
5. The core is made of graphite.
6. It's about 7 inches (~18cm) long.
7. It's about ¼ inch (~6mm) thick.
8. It has a rubber eraser at the end.
9. It's sold in bulk, and each pencil is only ~$0.25.

And here are some of the benefits those features provide:

1. The pencil is easy to notice on a messy desk because it's usually the only yellow thing on it.
2. It creates easy-to-read text, and it's smooth to write with.

3. It makes working faster and easier since the eraser is attached, so you won't get distracted from writing if you don't have an eraser handy.
4. It can easily be re-sharpened to ensure crisp writing.
5. It's lightweight and therefore easy to write with even for long periods, but it's also durable so you don't have to worry about it breaking.
6. Unlike a pen's ink, pencil washes off clothes and hands if you get smudged.
7. Even if you sharpen it several times a day, the pencil has a long writing life.
8. It's comfortable to hold as you write.
9. It's cost effective and, even if you lose one, you don't need to run to the store if you buy in bulk.

Which of these benefits are actually most important depend on your target customers. But by creating a list like this, identifying the most important benefits for any product is easier.

Don't Blend In-Stand Out From The Competition

Your product or service has to be great for your target customers. That is, it has to offer great benefits.

But that's not enough.

If you don't stand out from your competition, people won't notice you or believe that your product or service could be the best for them.

Being a "normal," "safe," or "average" choice doesn't work in business. Being "normal" might make you some personal friends. But if your business is "average," it's also trivial.

You have to somehow stand out from the competition, or your target customers won't believe you're the best choice for them.

Let's say you're looking for a photographer for your wedding. You find 10 photographers who offer services from baby's first birthday and holiday pics of the kids to family reunions –and, of course, weddings. They're "normal" photographers, and they'd all be happy to take your money and take your wedding photos.

And then you find one who specializes in weddings.

Assuming budget isn't a factor and all other things are equal, who do you call?

Now let's say you need a photographer when you're selling your house. Do you even consider the "normal" photographers, or do you go straight to those who specialize in real estate photography?

Sure, the "normal" photographers probably get some wedding and real estate work. But not often, not easily, and not for a good fee.

When people don't specialize in a specific area, it's usually because they're worried they'll miss out on opportunities. They're afraid of being the wedding photographer who never gets asked to take pictures of homes for sale or anything but weddings.

But even if you're contacted by only 1% of potential customers, that's more than the 0% you'd get if you didn't specialize.

Being a great choice for 1% is much better than being a mediocre choice for 100%.

That said, the wedding photographer still has many competitors (or at least it's possible that dozens of other wedding photographers are readily available). But standing out from the direct competition means getting attention–and the sales.

For example, maybe you, the potential client, would prefer a photographer who's focused on taking very artistic photos. You'd like your wedding photos to be 50% capturing the moment and 50% art.

This not only narrows your choices, it also means that finding your photographer depends on their specialization within wedding photography, their marketing, and their value proposition.

If one wedding photographer focuses on taking wedding photos with artistic value, you'd pick them over all the other "normal" wedding photographers.

However, another potential client who'd rather get happy, candid wedding photos wouldn't pick that photographer. Instead, they'd pick a wedding photographer who focuses on capturing the joy of the event.

But your specialty and focus aren't the only ways to stand out from your competition.

You can differentiate your business in countless ways. You probably already have aspects of your business that can make you stand out if you identify them and make them clear in your marketing.

Keep in mind that seemingly irrelevant aspects can actually be surprisingly differentiating. For example, if you're the only woman among the local men's tailors, that fact differentiates you. It doesn't really matter in any serious way. But you can use it to your advantage and stand out from the competition.

You can also stand out with aspects that aren't unique to you if pointing them out makes you *seem* unique to your target customers. For example, maybe no other online writing coach advertises editing services even though they do editing in addition to coaching. Being the only one who markets that as a benefit can make you stand out if you present it effectively.

Finding the most useful differentiating aspects of your business can be challenging, and there's no quick way of doing it. But here's a question that often helps: What has made your current and past customers choose you?

If you pose that question to your customers, most answers won't be useful because few people are conscious of the reasoning behind their choices. But sometimes you'll get an answer you can use in your marketing, and it's more than worth the time and effort of asking the question.

Make Sure Your Marketing Is Believable

The best, most persuasive reason to do something is completely irrelevant if people don't believe it's true.

We learn to doubt marketing before we're old enough for school. Unless the marketing hits the sweet spot just right–and "everyone" has that product–we instinctively wonder if a claim is somehow misleading or only partly true.

Your target customers will rarely think you're outright lying. But they aren't confident that all your claims are completely honest either. And for good reason; many business owners aren't concerned with honesty nearly as much as they are with sales.

But there's no real need for misleading anyone in marketing–assuming your product or service is actually valuable.

Consider this carefully:

It's generally easier to make people believe an honest claim than to make them believe a lie. And when people believe you, they're much more likely to buy from you.

But since people will doubt your claims even if you're honest, you have to know how to convince them that you and your marketing really are honest.

Customer testimonials are the most common evidence of truth that marketers rely upon. But even though testimonials are usually beneficial, they're not always the best way to convince potential customers.

Simply put, you can prove your claims in five ways:

1. **Rely on your own words.** Just hope that people will believe you when you say something. In many situations, and especially if you're already established as an authority, your word is all people need. But in at least as many situations, especially if you're just starting out, your words aren't enough.

2. **Rely on other people's words**. Use testimonials and endorsements to back up your credibility and the claims you make.

3. **Rely on facts and research**. If your target customers aren't skeptical about research and studies, they're likely to believe claims that are backed up with facts and research references.

4. **Give results in advance**. Just like food brands sometimes give free samples at grocery stores, let your potential customers "taste" your product before paying for it. By offering a free chapter of an ebook or a free trial of a course, for example, people can get some of the results your products and services create–and want more.

5. **Be "intuitively true."** This is the trickiest but possibly the most useful way to prove your claims. Much like debating philosophers create chains of arguments that negate questions and objections, you can present your claims in such a way that your target customers won't see any need to question or doubt the logic of what you say. If you do that successfully, then the claim is intuitively true.

Some claims just can't be made no matter what the evidence is.
First, people won't believe a claim that your product or service is "the best." For example, they won't believe that the bicycle you sell is "the best bicycle."

But you have to be able to say–honestly–that your product or service is the best in some specific way, for a specific need, for specific kinds of people, or in some specific situation. Why else would people buy it?

And when you're specific about how your product is better than all the rest, people will believe it. You still need to present and prove the claims effectively, but that can be learned.

Second, people won't believe a claim that states your product is "cutting edge" or "the industry leader" unless they already believe those things about your company, products, or services. The problem with those and similar claims is that they're clichés. They're old, they're tired, and they're overused. They've lost meaning because so many companies claim their products are cutting edge and that they're the industry leader–but only one company can be the industry leader, after all, and which one is it?

So, when you've formulated the ideas that you want people to believe–what will persuade them to pay attention to you and buy from you–consider whether you can actually persuade people to believe those ideas.

If people won't easily believe something, it's not a claim you should make in your marketing, especially early on. At least you shouldn't focus on it.

Focus Your Marketing on Your Value Proposition

Realistically, your prospective customer can understand and believe only a few claims right away. If the claims are unusually simple and clearly connected to each other, four or five might work.

But in most cases, you should focus on only three ideas. In other words, you should focus your marketing on the three most persuasive reasons your target customers should pay attention to your products or services and buy.

Those three reasons form your value proposition.

Fewer than three highly persuasive reasons are unlikely to be enough to make your marketing effective. And trying to communicate more than that is likely to dilute your message, and people won't understand or believe any of the reasons.

When your marketing makes people understand the most persuasive reasons for them to pay attention to you and your products and services and buy, your marketing is as effective as it can be.

You can eventually focus on other benefits and reasons to buy your product or service. But initially, your objective should be communicating your value proposition in a way that makes people interested in learning more. And almost everything in your marketing should somehow relate or refer to the key concepts in your value proposition.

Plus, when all your marketing includes your value proposition, everyone who encounters your marketing efforts will immediately self-qualify. That means if they're your target customers, they'll immediately see why they should pay attention. If they aren't your target customers, well, then what they do doesn't matter.

As long as you focus on your value proposition, you'll get results with any marketing tactic–sales pages, videos, podcasts, social media, and so on–that gets your message in front of your target customers. Even if you're not a master of the particular marketing tactic, you can still communicate the key ideas, get people interested, and make sales.

When you have a clear value proposition and include it in all your marketing efforts, growing your business is much easier and faster.

You'll know exactly what to say in your marketing, you don't need to use all the different marketing tactics and tools, and you won't waste time and effort on ideas that won't make any real difference.

There's nothing magical or secret about what makes some business owners successful; they just give people great reasons to buy their products, and people are thrilled and even proud to do it.

If you'd like to find out whether your ideas will work in your marketing–how persuasive they are–use this free, 5-step exercise that quickly lets you evaluate your ideas with almost uncomfortable honesty: **http://www.petersandeen.com/exercise/**

About Peter Sandeen

Peter Sandeen dreams of sailing with his wife and dogs when he's not helping businesses stand out from the competition with value proposition marketing. Find out what makes people want to pay attention to you and buy your products and services–download the quick 5-step exercise that shows the core of your value proposition.

CHAPTER 4

More Enquiries From Your Website

Nick Jervis

Simple Changes To Instantly Generate More Enquiries Without Increasing Your Marketing Spend

Most business owners I meet are really good at fulfilling the service that they provide. However, when it comes to being as busy as they would like or want to be, that is often a completely different matter.

As a marketing man, my focus is always on 'automatic client attraction'; that is, putting in place automated marketing systems which take place with or without the business owner's input. This is absolutely vital if you are to once and for all get off 'the marketing rollercoaster'.

The marketing roller coaster looks like this (beautifully illustrated I think you will agree):

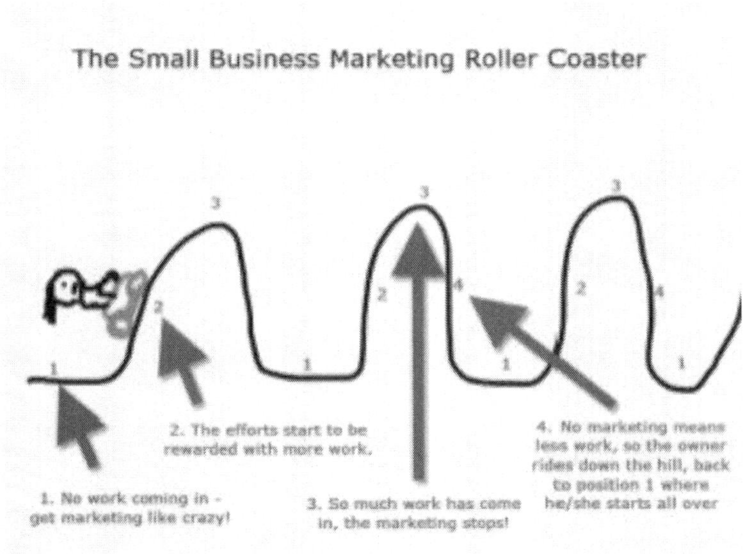

Whilst the image may not be that recognisable to you (or memorable for that matter), the story behind it may well be familiar.

As an entrepreneur, you are at your best when you are providing your specialist service and looking after your clients. However, from time to time, you do not have enough clients to care for.

So you do a lot of marketing, make a lot of noise and slowly but surely you start to generate some new clients for your business (position 2 in the image above). This is good, as you are now doing what you love to do. Sadly, however, as you become busier and busier, you reach a point when you are so busy looking after your clients that all of the marketing you were doing stops (position 3).

This is fine whilst you are still busy taking care of the clients generated by your last marketing activity, but after a while you notice that you have more time on your hands as you reach and go past position 4.

Soon you are back at position 1, back to where you started. This is not good. There is no new work coming in and you start to panic. How are you going to pay the bills? Will you be able to keep trading?

You frantically start marketing your services again, pushing your roller coaster back up the hill as fast as you can in an effort to generate some more clients. You tell yourself that you won't make this mistake again, but sadly as you become busier again, exactly the same thing happens again, and then again, and again. You are now well and truly on the marketing roller coaster!

If you really want your business to grow and pass this vicious cycle, you absolutely have to put in place some automated marketing systems so that clients come to you without the need for your regular marketing input.

That is why my section focuses on one of the easiest and most successful methods for entrepreneurs to generate enquiries for their services automatically; their website.

If you have been in business for any period of time, your website will already be attracting visitors who are interested in your services, yet many of them will not go make contact with you.

Whilst the average figures suggest that for every 100 visitors to your website, two will get in touch with you, the reality is that for many of the 100's of websites that I have analysed over the years the actual figure is well below 1%. Despite people finding your website when they have a pressing need for your service, they leave before taking any action. Why is this, and what difference would it make to your business and profits if you could change your own figure to 2, 3 or even 5%?

It is because this area can dramatically change the success of your business very quickly, yet with little or no cost whatsoever, that I am focusing on it.

So, let's crack on with some simple changes you can make to your website to increase the volume of people asking you to help them.

1. How Much is EAMWYDYTOM Costing You?

EAMWYDYTOM (*'oo moody tom'* as I like to call it with a large dose of poetic licence) usually costs entrepreneurs a fortune.

If we were both at a networking event, or more interestingly a cocktail party, EAMWDYTOM would be the person who runs towards you, thrusts their business card into your hands, talks about what they do, how brilliant they are, and why you should be grateful to know them, before bustling off to do the same again with their next unfortunate victim.

I prefer meeting this sort of person at a networking event because then at least I know I will be free from them within an hour, whereas at a cocktail party it could be many hours.

When it comes to your website, are you making this mistake?

Enough

About
Me
What
Do
You
Think
Of
Me

If your website starts by talking all about you or your business, before talking more about your business and ending with why your business is so great, you need to spend some time turning your content around to be all about your clients.

My simple marketing definition is important here:

Clients First!

Everything on your website has to put your clients' needs and interests first.

By way of an example, rather than a website saying this:

Jenkins & Co were established in 1838 and have been providing exceptional financial planning services ever since. We have won countless awards and believe that you will not find more expert knowledge anywhere else.

It must say something more like this, turning every feature of your service into a tangible benefit for your clients:

We realise that everyone has different needs, which is why we start by finding out all about you before providing you with any recommendations. Our initial 'fact finding' call is completely free of charge, and requires absolutely no form filling on your part. It is our duty to make the often challenging business of putting your finances in order to make this process as easy and pain free as possible for you.

If you are in need of financial planning advice, we would be delighted to use all of our experience, gained since 1838 to provide the best advice to suit your circumstances.

Action Points

Look at each page of your website now and make sure you are not making the EAMWDYTOM mistake. If you are, changing this can instantly increase the volume of enquiries that you receive.

2. What Sort Of Leads Should You Be Targeting?

Is that a strange question? I realise that it might seem so, but let me explain what I mean.

If you have sought any marketing advice before now, you will often see many 'marketing gurus' recommending that you offer something free of charge on your website in return for your prospect's email address. You can then follow up with an automated email marketing system unless or until that prospect is ready to buy your services. This is called 'lead generation' marketing.

The trouble is that this is not the correct form of marketing for every type of business, so you need to know whether it is right for you.

With this in mind, I have created a simple formula, based on having tested this across many different service businesses:

1. If you sell services which have an air of urgency around them, you should target an 'instant contact' response (see later in this chapter). In this case your prospect has a very annoying and pressing 'itch' which needs scratching quickly and they have no idea how to go about scratching it

themselves. They need an expert to do it for them. Types of services that should target 'instant contact' leads will include accountants, solicitors/lawyers, insurance brokers etc.

2. If you sell services which people need to discover more about over a period of time, you should target lead generation. These people have an itch, but they are not yet sure if they need someone to scratch it for them, whether it will go away in its own time or whether they can work out how to scratch it themselves. Services falling into this category will include business like business continuity consultants, marketing consultants, coaches etc.

There will be exceptions, and the best way to find out which is right for you is to test it, but by and large, the above works well.

My question for you is this; have you been targeting the right kind of leads?

Action Points

If you have been targeting 'lead generation' for some time and are getting no results, add an enquiry form and you may find that you instantly start to receive enquiries for your services. See the section below entitled 'How Can I Get In Touch?' to discover more.

3. What Is It That You Do?

We now move into some really simple, quick fixes that can have a dramatic impact on the volume of enquiries that you generate from your website literally overnight.

Here is the first one.
When I land on your website, can I tell within 10 seconds exactly what it is that you do? In other words, do you spell out the service that you provide immediately beneath your logo?
If not, you are losing business.

Why? Well, your future clients are the same as all of us; that is completely starved of time and wanting, expecting and deserving that you make their life as easy as possible for them.

If you do not make it abundantly clear what you do immediately beneath your logo you will have people hitting the back button in no time at all and moving on to your competitors' websites.

I cannot tell you the number of times I have had to hunt around a website trying to work out what the business is all about. This is simply unacceptable.

So tell me what you do. If you are a solicitor/lawyer, say so. A marketing consultant, tell me. An accountant, shout it out loud and proud.

Just make sure you don't leave me guessing, as I won't stay around long enough to play that game.

Action Points

Check your own website now and make sure that you are making it abundantly clear, immediately beneath your logo, the service that you provide.

4. What Is It You Want Me To Do?

If I manage to find your website on a Google search, click through to your website, see that you provide the service I am looking for as you cleverly say so immediately beneath your logo, will you then tell me what I should do to take matters to the next stage, or will you completely leave me hanging?

Most websites that I visit sadly make the mistake of leaving me hanging. You might think that this is not important.

"There is a contact page Nick, so go there and you will find out what to do next. Don't be so lazy."

However, if you think that, you are definitely throwing away thousands in terms of lost profits for your business, possibly even tens of thousands.

Most people will visit only one to three pages on your website. Therefore, every page of your website has to work as hard as possible to ensure that your visitor can complete their journey around your website in as short a number of clicks as possible.
This means that when they reach the bottom of a page on your website, you should tell them exactly what they need to do next to take matters forward.
If you are an 'instant itch' business, the bottom of your page might look something like this:

Make A Free Enquiry

Call us now on 01234 5678990, email us on info@businessname.co.uk or complete our Instant Online Enquiry (linking to your enquiry form).

If you sell a 'slow itch' service, it might look like this:

8 Ways To Instantly Attract Clients

Download my free guide showing you 8 methods which are working right now to instantly generate new clients for your business.

Name field:
Email field:

(This is the method I use from my Small Business Salt marketing website - a definite slow itch service).

Action Points
Go and check the bottom of each page of your website now. If you are not making it easy for your visitors to get in touch at the bottom of every single page, fix this quickly.

5. How Can You Persuade Me To Do It?

When I land on your website, on average, you have less than two minutes to persuade me that I should get in touch with you. Are you making the most of this two minute period?

If I am going to get in touch with you, I am going to have to provide some contact details. Before I go to this trouble, you need to win me over and show me that you are someone I can trust with these details.

To help you to persuade more people that you are indeed worthy of this trust, as I am sure you are, I have created the 'Two Minute Trust Builder', providing you with a process to follow to win your website visitors' trust in this short period of time.

The Two Minute Trust Builder (TMTB) is split into two parts:

Depth of expertise; and
Endorsements of expertise.

Let's look at each of these in turn.

Depth Of Expertise
There are two ways you must prove that you have the sufficient depth of expertise to win me over, and these are as follows:

By having sufficient content on each page (at least 400 words); and

By having a good number of pages within each of your services sections to show that you provide this service on a regular basis.

Both are equally important. If I am looking for an accountant for a business, yet there is just one page selling all of your accountancy services, I am unlikely to be convinced that you are the right business for me. There is simply no depth of content to prove your expertise.

Likewise, if you only have one or two paragraphs on a page about the service I am interested in, how am I supposed to believe that you really are an expert?

Remember what I said above, most people will only visit between one to three pages on your website. You have to do all that you can on every single page to persuade them that your business is the right one for their needs.

If you need help with a formula for each page, I am going to provide my Copywriting Template in the resources section at the end of this chapter for you, as I only have so much space in this chapter, and I have a lot more information that I want to provide for you.

Endorsements Of Expertise

It is one thing to say that you are the right business for my needs, but your visitors will be even more impressed when there are external endorsements of your expertise. Do you have them?

These will include:

- Any relevant qualifications;
- Testimonials;
- Press coverage;
- Books published; and
- Volume of people/businesses that you have helped with your services.

You can easily include these in a box on the right hand side of your website under a heading "Why Choose Me/Us" linking through to a page with more of an explanation about each of the points covered above (or to a page with hundreds of testimonials about your services - don't stop at only six testimonials like every other business does).

Action Points

Do you have enough content on each page, and enough pages in each of your main services sections to show your visitors that you really are an expert?

Do you have external endorsements of your expertise, easily visible on each and every page of your website?

6. How Can I Get In Touch?

If you manage to get me to the point that I am persuaded you are worthy of my contact details, do you provide me with a range of contact options?

All people are different, which means that whilst some people will be happy to call you straight away, others will prefer to email, but some will prefer another option, a contact form.

You might think that this is unnecessary, but when I tell you that it was only after I added an enquiry form to each page of my legal services website, www.1stclaims.co.uk, that enquiries spiralled upwards making me realise that I had been missing countless enquiries before taking this action.

We have spent hundreds of thousands of pounds promoting this website, so trust me when I tell you that you need an enquiry form on each and every page of your website or you will be missing a lot of enquiries for your services.

Don't make the same mistake that I made.

Mobile Browsers

I mentioned above that some people will be happy to call you, as indeed they will. Now when you bear in mind that traffic from mobile devices is increasing exponentially, you really have to make it as easy as possible for visitors to call you.

The good news is that you can now make every telephone number on your website instantly dial-able by the mobile browser simply clicking it to call you. All you need is a simple piece of website coding which I am going to provide you with in the resources section.

Action Points

If you do not yet have an enquiry form on each and every page of your website, or at least a link to it, fix this immediately. If you are targeting lead generation, make the enquiry form your lead generation offer.

Link your telephone number using the Mobile Phone code I am providing for you in the resources section to make it as easy as possible for mobile phone users to contact you.

7. How Can You Make It Sexier?

Now that we know each other a little better, I have a small confession to make. I am a huge lover of Apple. I know this will please some of you, but annoy others, but let me explain why.

Apple are absolutely genius when it comes to marketing, so being a marketing man, I find that really quite interesting.

The good news for you is that you can copy some of their genius and use it for your own advantage, just like I did to receive a 50% spike in enquiries for my services.

First, let me explain what they do so well.

For years we have all had the technical ability to make video calls, they just weren't very sexy (and mostly didn't work). Along came Apple with Face Time, and suddenly everyone you see is walking into objects and people whilst holding their phone at arm's length because they are having some 'Face Time'.

High Definition has been around for many years, but Retina Eye Display sounds so much more appealing, so I want it right now!

Finally, we have had computer programmes for many years. I use lots of computer programmes. They all serve a purpose very well. I use them every day. However, I don't particularly love them.

But give me an 'App' on my Macbook or iPhone and suddenly I am a very 'Appy' boy.

So what has this got to do with your products or services?

Do you want to sell something that everyone else is selling and call it by the same name, or do you want to sell something which is completely and utterly unique to your business, making it both more desirable and harder to compare to your competitors' offerings?

I told you that I had used this to get a 50% increase in one of my offerings, and this offering leads to the majority of my consultancy business. The offering is a very simple, yet valuable, free call with me to discuss your marketing.

Naturally, for a long time it was called a 'Free Call', and it worked just fine. I had two problems with it though:

- It had 'free' in the title, and in my experience people rarely attach value to anything that is free; and
- It wasn't unique.

So, after considering Apple's marketing prowess, I changed the name initially to "Marketing Strategy Call" and saw a slight increase. However, when I changed the name to include a benefit to the clients, it was then that I saw an overnight 50% increase in take up. The name change was to "More Clients Strategy Call" and this is when it really took off. Now the name was all about what my clients would receive from this call, and it was unique to my business.

I will keep testing different names, but I hope the point is clear to you. You must name each aspect of your services to increase appeal to your prospects, and that name should include a benefit which your clients will receive from your offering.

Action Points

If you currently offer a free call, free initial meeting or a tester product, provide each of these services with a name that is completely unique to your business and conveys a benefit that your client will receive and you will instantly see an increase in take up.

8. How Will This Help You?

I know that the information in this chapter can make a substantial difference to the volume of enquiries that you receive from your website. I know this because I have already worked with businesses in many, many different sectors and applied these changes and seen increases in enquiries for their services.

Many of the changes might seem simple, but I always find that all the best ideas are.

The only thing that matters for you is whether they will work for you.

There Is No Treasure Without Measure

When you apply these changes, you absolutely must measure their success for two reasons:

- It shows you that the time taken to make the changes was very worthwhile; and
- It motivates you to make more changes.

So many business owners fail to measure their statistics and so do not see the improvements that they have made, which is a shame.

I have worked with businesses who have made these changes, then implied that they have not made any noticeable difference. When I go through their statistics and see that it has increased their enquiries by 20-50% they are usually completely gobsmacked and then desperate to make even more improvements.

There really is 'no treasure without measure', so please do one thing for me.

Action Points

- Measure the performance of your website for one month now, including:

    - Monthly visits to your website
    - Number of enquiries
    - Conversion rate (enquiries/visitors x 100)
    - Number of new clients from enquiries
    - Conversion rate (clients/enquiries x 100)

- Make the changes discussed above;
- Do the same measurement for the next three months.

When you see that improvement, as I am certain you will, please let me know.

Resources For You

I have a host of resources for you to help you to automate your marketing and make your life so very much easier, so please head over to the resources page below, add your details and instantly gain access to all of the following:

- How to write a website page that answers all of your prospects' questions, takes away any concerns or worries and ensures that more clients contact you from your website (**My Successful Copywriting Checklist**);

- The **Mobile Telephone Code** you need to copy and paste into your website that instantly allows website visitors using a mobile device to tap it to call you without having to enter your telephone number;

- **Automatic Client Attraction Software** that is invaluable in terms of helping you to generate more leads from your website and provide countless ideas for your future blog posts; and

- Entry into a monthly draw to win a free **Website New Client Explosion** video review (usually £295).

Simply head over to www.SmallBusinessSalt.co.uk/book and download these resources instantly and get yourself into the monthly **Website New Client Explosion** video review draw.

My Parting Thought

There is a saying that I use which many business owners have told me has allowed them to go from doing moderately well when growing their business to doing dramatically well.

When it comes to marketing, it needs quite a bit of pushing to get going, and most business owners struggle to push for as long or as hard as they need to.

You see marketing needs momentum, and often for most business owners that I work with, because they provide a service of a very high quality, they feel that their marketing must be 'perfect' too before they get it to work for them.

Nothing could be further from the truth with marketing.

Marketing needs momentum - Perfection Kills Momentum!

Just get going with your marketing, improve it as and when you can. But never, ever, wait for it to be perfect, it doesn't need to be to start working for you.

A bad website live today is one million times better than a perfect website published in 10 years' time (by which time you might have had to close your business). Remember this at all times:

Perfection Kills Momentum

Action Points

Make these changes to your website and you will be able to help more clients sooner than you think.

About Nick Jervis

Nick understands that most business owners are great at the service they provide, but not necessarily so good at marketing their services, so he teaches 'Automatic Client Attraction'.

"Letting the clients come to you as opposed to hunting them down means that you can grow your business with or without your daily input into your marketing, allowing you to focus on what you do best; looking after your clients."

Nick Jervis is a former solicitor (attorney/lawyer) who, since leaving the law has spent more than £2 million marketing his own service business websites to generate clients.

He uses everything he has learned, both good and bad, to help his marketing consultancy clients grow their businesses quickly and efficiently.

No nonsense, practical advice that you can implement easily and cost effectively.

You can see more at **http://www.smallbusinesssalt.co.uk/**

CHAPTER 5

The Proven 6 Step Formula Used By Successful Entrepreneurs To Generate Leads, Gain Their Trust, and Convert Them Into Lifetime Buyers

Jason “Wally” Waldron

Today’s environment for the entrepreneur looking to grow his business is more competitive than ever before. You're competing for eyeballs, you're competing for attention, and studies show that the vast majority of the

people you're trying to reach are more distracted than ever before.
Add to this the fact that the Internet moves so fast and every day the speed of business continues to increase. At the same time, the entrepreneur who is looking to find more clients is faced with an environment where your prospects are constantly bombarded with thousands of messages, distractions and conflicting messages from all directions.

In this environment, how do you stand out in the crowd, differentiate yourself, and get your clients to seek you out - rather than you having to hunt them down again and again?

You read this chapter.

In the competitive landscape of the Internet environment, you may have found yourself wondering if the "little guy" entrepreneur can still make it. I understand what you're experiencing, and I'm here today to tell you that YES, You Can. I understand how hard it can be to grow your business on the Internet. In fact, over 7 long years ago, I was in your shoes.

Working as a frustrated corporate IT guy, at night and on the weekends (and even during my lunches) I would struggle to put the pieces of a real, consistently

working business together and achieve freedom from the shackles of the "daily grind".
For years, it seemed like I tried everything and got nowhere. Subscribing to every newsletter under the sun. Reading blogs by "so called" experts. Buying books, taking courses, spending way too much money on the wrong investments and coaches while hoping and praying that I was getting closer to my goal.

Nothing really changed though, until I discovered the Proven 6 Step Formula used by successful entrepreneurs to generate leads, gain their trust, and convert them into lifetime buyers.

Think about it this way: There is a hidden order to everything in the Universe. And just as there is a structure to every atom in a molecule, there is a hidden, proven path followed by every successful Entrepreneur and Business Owner who has come before you. Following this path is what has made them successful.

By carefully studying what has worked for the successful entrepreneurs who've come before you, and what has worked for them to find and convert customers, you'll have the roadmap to generating more and more buyers that you can use in your own business.

Here's the great news. You don't have to spend years of studying or searching...I've done it for you.

Imagine holding this "secret roadmap" in your hands, as the previously hidden structure of your profitable business unfolds before your very eyes. Imagine seeing your strategy map for profits on the Internet created right in front of you, accessible at any time, where you finally understand how all the pieces fit together, as your actions are magically guided by this roadmap, and what was once "Difficult" now is "Easy"...

Introducing The Master Key Formula™ - The Most Powerful Marketing Formula Ever Discovered

The Master Key Formula™ consists of 6 proven "gears" that work in harmony with each other as a machine to attract qualified leads, nurture and education them while you build trust automatically, and then profit for the long term as you continue to bring value to your customers. In fact, as you go along and learn about this powerful formula, you will find that every successful entrepreneur who is using the Internet to grow is using a version of this formula in their business.

Join me as I show you how to insert the Master Key Formula™ into your business, and unlock previously hidden sales and profits.

The Master Key Formula™ consists of 6 distinct components:

1. The Traffic Stack
2. The Relationship Enhancers
3. The Prospect Siphon
4. The Trust Building Automated Follow Up Sequence
5. The Irresistible Offer
6. The Profit Maximizer

Many business owners have one or two of these items in place already. However, when you have all of them working in concert, the results can be quite impressive, and quite lucrative.

Let's talk about each component, and how you can insert each one into your business to see additional growth.

Part 1: The Traffic Stack

Getting traffic to your website is paramount to your success. After all, your traffic is where your leads and prospects come from.

When someone types in a problem they're looking to solve into the search engines, they're predisposed to be looking for solutions. Positioned well, you can be at the top of those key phrases, and be positioned as the perfect solution to their problem.

Recently, a client of mine informed me that two simple words that he's worked to achieve a number one ranking for, will be worth over $200k in business to him over the next 2-3 years. Not bad for a few hours invested in ranking for the right keywords.

It's important to remember 90% of the success of a company has absolutely nothing to do with your product or service. It has everything to do with your marketing. So getting a consistent flow of leads is important. Don't be alarmed - it's not all expensive, and it's not all SEO driven.

In today's environment, traffic is often more simple than you think to attract. The mistake most companies make is that they believe that they have stack every kind of traffic available, and that they're going to be able to get traffic for free.

That is 100% not the case. You don't have to stack every type of traffic.

I have worked with hundreds of companies 1 on 1, and many of them have traffic that comes from different areas. However, the most successful companies have learned to get traffic in a couple of key areas. Some of them get traffic only one way.

But to give you an idea of the most consistent sources of traffic, here is a list that I have found that brings in the most leads and prospects:

Blog Traffic
SEO (Search Engine Optimization)
Content Marketing
Article Writing
Trade Shows
Networking
Referral and Affiliate Partners
Joint Ventures
Email Marketing
Ad Retargeting
You Tube
Podcasting
Offline Lead Generation

...and there are many more. The key is that you start with one or two that work, and then add more as you start to see success. The other key, is to understand that traffic is an investment. It's always going to be either an investment of capital, or an investment of time, or both.

The great part is when done correctly, you can expect to achieve an endless stream of prospects to your business. No more scratching your head, feeling lost on the internet, wishing that you had access to the steady flow of customers coming to your business. Instead, you'll have floods of traffic every single day.

With a properly implemented traffic stack, you can expect to dominate the search engines and make Google your traffic slave, spitting out red hot prospects at will. With the right strategy, you can recruit an army of referral partners sending you heaps of clients ready and willing to buy. You can even gain an unfair advantage over your competition with the virtually unknown website formula that will use your competitor's websites against themselves. Yes, there is a way to ethically funnel your competition's hard earned traffic to your own offers.

It starts with knowing what you can achieve. 90% of the success of your website has absolutely nothing to do with your product or service. It has everything to do with your marketing and your traffic. Getting a consistent flow of leads is the first step to success.

Resource
If you'd like to increase your organic traffic to your website and achieve a **#1 Ranking** In Google's Search Results With Minimal Effort, visit:
http://wallythewebguy.com/seo/

Part 2: The Relationship Enhancers

All successful business happens because of a conversation based on relationships and trust. Successful marketing leads to sales only when your prospects value your relationship with them. Now that you've built a traffic stack, it's important to begin to start, and then nurture the relationship.

A good relationship enhancer will automatically position you as the valued expert, as the trusted resource, and as the "go to" solution. This serves to allow you to escape having to "sell" people on you, your product or service. More importantly, it serves to allow your own escape from poverty inducing "race to the bottom" low end pricing strategies.

Examples of relationship enhancers include:

- Case Studies
- 3rd Party Endorsements or 3rd Party Verified Results

- Video and Written Testimonials From Clients

A well written case study, of how you and your unique process took a customer from point A to point B, and how the prospect can do the same by working with you, is one of the most important pieces of collateral you can have in your business. As a consultant or practitioner, the transformation you can create for your clients is where the value you bring to the table resides.

3rd Party Verified results can be very useful, especially if you're selling something to analytical, skeptical buyers. Recently I saw a coach who was selling a trading system that is out of the box. He had a 3rd Party auditor verify that his student success rate is 92%. That's a very powerful relationship enhancer and trust builder for people who are on the fence about whether to trust him.

Video testimonials are a powerful testament to you, and what you bring to the table. They can't be faked, for the most part. And they tap into the proven concept of offering social proof by having others share how you've helped them.

One weird trick to help you create more effective video testimonials: Before you have somebody do a video testimonial for you, get them excited and laughing.

Jump up and down, have them jump up and down - have a little fun! The energy will come across in the video, and help them avoid being "camera shy".

Do these simple, yet high leverage things to put your relationship enhancers in place, and you'll find it's easier to charge a premium price over your competition, even if you're selling comparable goods or services. You'll likely also find that you've gained credibility in your market as the "go to" source. Ultimately, relationship enhancers help you be positioned to close more sales at higher ticket prices, with less effort than you've ever done before.

Part 3: The Prospect Siphon

92% of people come to a website one time and never return. The third component of the Master Key Formula™ solves this.

Because of today's environment where it's a never ending competition for eyeballs and attention, it's more essential than ever that you collect your prospect's information and follow up with them. The alternative is to let your competition snatch them up.

The prospect siphon is a valuable way of enticing prospects to give you their name and email address with the permission of sending them more information that will bring them closer to a sale. You've probably heard of the term "lead magnet". A lead magnet is how you entice people to come through your prospect siphon, via a targeted landing page.

You've probably been on the type of page that offers a free e-book, whitepaper, or video presentation - whereby you trade your information in return for access to the information. This is called permission marketing, and it's proven to be much more measurable and effective than other forms of marketing.
In fact, your competition is likely clueless about this type of marketing.

According to Hubspot Inbound Marketing:

"Too many companies send their email, social media, and search traffic to their homepages. This is the equivalent of throwing leads away. You could capture these leads at a much higher rate simply by sending them to targeted landing pages."
(Source: Pamela Vaughan, Hubspot Inbound Marketing)

Simply having a prospect siphon and collecting leads will put you far ahead of the majority of your competitors. Now that you're capturing leads and building your list, it's time to convert these leads into customers, without as much effort on your part. That's what the next section is about.

Part 4: The Trust Building Automated Follow Up System

Studies show 90% of transactions are done on the 5-12th contact with your prospect, so now that you've captured their information, it's important to follow up.

The key, as I always say, is to leave nothing to chance. And that means, "When in doubt, automate it out!".

Without it, you'll lose most of the business that should have been yours.

Most people don't have a system of follow up that will drive a sale. One of the most important, and often overlooked elements of your Money Making Website is your "Trust Building Automated Follow Up System" or "T.B.A.F.S.".

It's important to have your follow up automated.

Smart entrepreneurs learn how to leverage technology to help them in their sales process. Having a trust building automated follow up system in place will allow you to automate your pre-sales process. Without this, you will be a slave to manual follow up and will never get off the hamster wheel.

On the other hand, if you have this part automated, it's like cloning yourself again and again. Let's fast forward and say that you have a well developed series of trust building automated follow up emails that bring as many prospects as possible to your offers.

The question is, where do you send them?

The end goal is to get them to your Irresistible Offer Page.

Part 5: The Irresistible Offer

At this point you have your follow up automated, and you have people coming back to your site again and again. It's time to send them to your "Irresistible Offers".

Over the years I've seen countless offer pages, and not all of them are created equally. The ones that bring in floods of sales and profits have been crafted by marketing experts who have spent countless hours perfecting their craft.

However, there are a number of great ways to get good copy. At the end of this chapter, I'll share some resources that you can utilize. And truth be told, if you can afford to hire a great copywriter - hire him immediately - start making sales - and thank me later for the advice.

Now if you are on a budget that dictates you need to write your own copy (or create it in house), best practices such as doing market research, research of your competition, keyword research, and being in touch with the conversation that your market is already having in their head will all be important for you.

The first thing to do when writing an irresistible offer is to find out all of the pain points and emotional hot buttons that you can push. Ask yourself questions such as the following:

- Where is your prospects' pain?
- What keeps them up at night?
- Who are they angry at?
- Who has sold them something - or tried to - and how have they failed?

The beautiful thing about humanity is that we're all emotional beings who make decisions based purely on emotion. Then, once we've made an emotional decision, we turn around and use our logic to justify whatever emotional decision we just made. Yes, even business people.

Another beautiful thing about humanity is that we're each much more afraid of loss and motivated by the *fear* of loss than we're motivated by the promise of gain. Studies prove this.

These two insights are huge when you're crafting an irresistible offer. These are the buttons you want to push.

Now that you have traffic coming to your website, you've built the relationship with your customers, and they trust you as their perfect answer to their problems, it's time to maximize your profits. After all, without profits, you've got nothing, which brings us to...

Part 6: The Profit Maximizer

The profit maximizer is scientifically designed to generate as much revenue and profits possible for your business. This success of the Master Key in your business is highly dependent on your success with the Profit Maximizer.

This is an area that a lot of business owners neglect or forget about, however, you will only have a fraction of the success you deserve if you don't develop a Profit Maximizer system.

After all, it's not about how much you make (revenue), it's all about how much you keep (profits).

How you go about the profit maximizer depends on your business model, and it has three primary "gears": Your sales team, automated fulfillment, and customer service.

When these three "gears" are working together, you'll have a well oiled profit machine where you'll effectively upsell, crossell, and maintain long term customer loyalty. By treating customers well, interacting with them in a way that solves their problems, and helps them generate results, you increase the lifetime value of each customer. And smart entrepreneurs know that it's much easier to keep a happy customer than it is to acquire new ones.

There are a number of ways that you can successfully implement a profit maximizer.

Some companies prefer that customers purchase automatically through the Internet, and focus on upselling their customers quickly and easily by incorporating their money making website into the upsell process. This would be good for a coach, for instance, who had a group coaching program.

Other companies focus on having a sales team generate a purchase for a high ticket item. Others wish to fulfil using a highly involved customer fulfillment process designed to keep long term recurring customers, and upsell them from there.

Some companies do a combination of all of these...

The key to understand, is that with a profit maximizer in effect, you have a business designed to multiply profits from new and existing clients.

To create a profit maximizer, you first list all of the distance products and services you are selling.

Then, you consider the entry points that various clients arrive through.

Finally, you consider how to take "C.A.R.E." of the customer. This simple, but high leverage process goes like this:

C - Customer is acquired
A - Ask Them Questions
R - Recommend Ways You Can Help Further (Upsell/Cross Sell/Referral/Etc.)
E - Extend the Relationship

Take "C.A.R.E." of your customers and keep them for life, and they'll take care of you.

By applying the Master Key Formula™, you'll likely find that you have generated more leads, gained their trust, and converted them into lifetime buyers...ensuring you more profits than ever before.

About Jason "Wally" Waldron

Jason "Wally" Waldron, known as Wally the Web Guy, is an internationally recognized author and speaker who works with individuals and businesses worldwide to apply his "Master Key Formula™" to create a stampede of customers for you automatically via the internet.

Over the past few years he's helped numerous entrepreneurs how to unlock their true value and create millions in additional sales and profits. To discover the proven step by step methods to unlock your value and maximize your profits, visit:
http://internetsalesstampede.com/

CHAPTER 6

Conducting Live Events For Fun And Profit

Tom Zeeb

It's only an online world these days, right?

Wrong.

Parts of it are. But plenty of other parts are not.

Human beings still have a desire for real, actual, face-to-face interaction.

(And you could easily argue that people are actually craving in-person interaction, as they have been deprived of it through "social" media)

And that is why there is an excellent opportunity to build your business by hosting live events.

You will build your list, build your business, and profit handsomely.

If you do it right.

For a large part of the last decade, I've been an event producer for my own events and a speaker at other people's events.

This lets me reach a wider audience, position myself powerfully in my market, help more people, and boost my profits substantially.

You can do the same.

(And it's actually a lot of fun.)

Let's discuss how...

Your Events Position You

What industry are you in?

Pretty much every industry has training events and networking events for the people in their niche.

These events position the host(s) as experts in their field because they are seen as being in a position of authority.

Think about it... Who do you trust more?

The person you have never heard of, or the one who is on stage running an event for your industry?

The answer is obvious.

Being the leader of an event makes you the leader. And being the leader gives you authority and credibility. That will be good for your business as it will bring you more clients, more relationships, and more profits.

A well-run event reflects positively on you as well, as when people experience a well-run event it builds trust in you and your brand.

Pay close attention to the entire experience your attendees are having.

Does the location reflect favorably? Or is a cheap hotel ballroom? Spend the necessary time researching the venues available in your area. Get an idea of prices and become a great negotiator when it comes to dealing with the hotel or venue sales team.

Is your check in table well run? Is it smooth and efficient and confidence inspiring? Or is it a confusing mess?

Is your staff friendly and professional? Or clueless and rude?

Is your audio/visual setup crisp, clear, and reliable? Or do the microphones crackle, squeal, and cut-out?

Do you respect your start time and end time? Or do people know they can show up late?

If your competition isn't doing events, then you easily set yourself apart. And even if they are, a well-run event can distinguish you from them and put you ahead.

Filling The Room

If you just build it, will they come?

No.

It will take some focused work on your part to fill the room. (Shocking, isn't it?)

It all starts with having something that people actually want.

Read that last sentence again, as most people miss this very important point.

You have to be hosting an event on a subject that people actually want to learn more about. That's the very first step. If no one is interested, then no one will show up. So be sure you are choosing to focus on a topic that actually has some interest out there, or you will be frustrated by your lack of traction.

Once you have a topic, then you need to build a list.

Having a list of prospects gives you a chance to tell them more about you and your event so you can warm them up to actually buying a ticket.

Most people will not be ready to buy a ticket right away, so you need to warm them up first.

You need to have a website to advertise your event and this website needs to have a way of capturing people's contact information.

I'd just focus on getting their email address at first. This keeps it simple. If they leave your website without giving you their email, the chances are you will never have another opportunity with them again. So you simply have to capture their email on their first visit.
You do this by making them an offer they can't refuse. Provide some sort of bait that is irresistible to them. Something that they absolutely have to have, and the only way to get it is to trade their email address for it.

What exactly is that bait?

That's what you need to figure out. Think about a pain that your market has and then think about a solution to it. Then produce an audio recording or written "special report" of you discussing it and offer it in exchange for their email address. Be sure to come up with a catchy title that grabs their attention.

Now that you have their email address, send them a series of emails on a regular basis.

Design an email campaign that walks them through the various problems your market is having. The solution to each of these problems will be to buy a ticket to your event.

There is nothing wrong with that. You couldn't possibly solve all their problems in an email, so getting them to the event is the only real way of actually helping them. Therefore it is your responsibility to do all that you can to get them to buy a ticket.

Keep your emails short and to the point. People these days don't have a lot of time, and they get a lot of emails, so you need to stand out with interesting subject lines and then have pithy messages that don't take long to read.

Keep each message to just one simple topic. Don't overdo it. If you brainstorm out 17 different hot buttons that your market has, then write 17 different messages focused on each hot button one-by-one. Don't merge it all together and try to cover it all in one fell swoop. Save your ammunition and fire your shots one at a time.

The ongoing email "conversation" will build rapport with them and make them more likely to buy a ticket and attend your event.

But if you dump everything on them at once, they will tune out and never even consider attending.

You should be building your list offline as well, by attending networking events, or thinking through other people who have a following that would be interested in your topic and then approaching them and offering to joint venture.

Put these people into the same email sequence so that you can warm them up and get them ready to buy a ticket.

Charge Appropriately

Education is valuable.

Therefore it should be paid for.

People are paying absurd amounts of money for university educations these days. They pay for language classes, cooking classes, dance classes, and much more.

So why wouldn't you charge for your events?

If you are providing value and teaching them what they need to know to succeed in the field you specialize in, then you need to be charging.

Charging to attend is also a screening technique. It massively improves the quality of the attendees you will have. Because when people have to decide to spend their hard-earned money on something, they think through their decision carefully, then they commit to attending.

Your attendance show-up rate improves, and the sales at your event will be higher as well, as the person who has already invested to attend is more likely to invest in what you are offering at the event.

If you sell a product or service at your events (as you should), you still need to charge to attend. Don't think people are allergic to a sales pitch and therefore shouldn't have to pay. If what you are presenting is truly valuable, then giving them the option to invest to learn more is actually welcomed, not resented.

And remember that your entrance fees must cover your hotel/venue cost. You should be at least at break-even when the event starts from the proceeds of the ticket sales. This way you know you have all your expenses covered and the sales at the event are now your profits.

What To Capture At Each Event To Use For Marketing The Next Event

Take advantage of your current event by using it to produce marketing for future events.

There is no better time to develop marketing materials for you future events than at your current event.

Be sure to take photos of your room. People relate to seeing other people in attendance and it gives them a sense of what your events are like.

Remember, a stranger who comes across your website doesn't really know you yet, and the thought of showing up at an event is intimidating.

So being able to see photos and videos of your events makes it less scary to attend.

When someone sees smiling faces, nice people, and hears video testimonials about how valuable your events are, they are more likely to want to attend.

Photos and videos help break down the natural resistance to the unknown because it makes your events familiar even though they have yet to attend themselves.

Videos are the best way of capturing the testimonials you need.

Once you have a video, you can:

- Transcribe it to have written quotes for your printed materials, newsletter, and website.
- Pull freeze frames from it to have still images.
- Use it as a video on your website, on a promotional DVD, or put it into a video montage.

Don't worry about perfection when filming, just capture people raving about how great your event was for them. Ask them a leading question to frame what it is you are looking for them to say. Tell them to speak from the heart so that you can help others just like you helped them.

For example, have them say "As a result of this event I can now..." or "What I loved about this event is..."

People will naturally tell others about you and your events if they enjoyed it and learned something valuable from attending.

You should further encourage this by reaching out to your attendees and asking them to refer other people they think would benefit from what you have to offer.

Get Started!

Done correctly, hosting live events will massively build your brand, position yourself as the market leader, and produce an excellent revenue source. All while being fun in the process.

So if you aren't doing events in your business, you need to start today.

Remember, no matter how many times you click from place-to-place, it will never replace face-to-face.

To learn more about the events I produce, visit:

www.TractionREIA.com
www.TractionRealEstateMentors.com

I take on a select few consulting clients who want to build up their business through conducting events. If you would like to find out more and be considered for my coaching, email me on **tom@tomzeeb.com**

About Tom Zeeb

Tom Zeeb has been featured by CNBC, Kiplinger's Magazine, and The Washington Post, among others. Tom is a business mentor to entrepreneurs and real estate investors. He is the President of Traction Real

Estate Mentors and Traction REIA, the Recipient of the National REIA "Honors of Merit" and the "Award of Excellence" for Best Real Estate Investor Association!

CHAPTER 7

Google Adwords: Unlocking The Secrets Of Highly Effective Internet Advertising

Mike Seddon

Did you know that internet advertising is now one of the most popular advertising media in the world? Spending on internet advertising has exceeded all other forms of advertising including TV, radio and newspapers.

There are very good reasons why many businesses are putting more of their advertising budget into internet advertising. For one thing, the number of people you can reach is far greater than most other forms of advertising and it's usually far cheaper to reach all those people.

Another reason for its popularity is that it is far easier to measure success. When you advertise online, you can directly track how many people the advert brings to your website. You can even track how many sales or leads it generates. That isn't easy to do with other forms of advertising. In fact with most other forms of advertising, it's practically impossible to directly measure success. As Jon Wanamaker famously said nearly a century ago, "Half the money I spend on advertising is wasted. The trouble is I don't know which half." Most business continuing with advertising that isn't working because they aren't sure which bits to stop!

By far the best way to advertise on the internet is to use Pay Per Click advertising (often referred to as PPC). Unlike other forms of advertising, with PPC you do not pay for your adverts to be seen. You only pay when someone clicks on your adverts and comes to your website, hence the name "pay per click". You literally pay for each click (ie: visitor to your website).

This is one of the reasons PPC advertising is very attractive to many businesses. Why pay for an advert on TV or in a newspaper when the amount you pay is determined by the size of the viewing figures or the number of readers a newspaper claims it has? Surely what's important to you is how many visitors does the advertising send to your website and how many sales does it generate.

PPC advertising puts the power back into the hands of you, the business owner. When you can measure success based on your terms, then you can pick and choose your advertising to suit your needs.

Google Is The King Of Internet Advertising

The undisputed leader in PPC advertising is Google. You've seen their adverts every time you use Google. They run across the top of the screen and down the left hand side. Those adverts are PPC adverts and Google's advertising service is called Adwords.

You may have heard the "myth" that no one clicks on those adverts. Maybe you are one of the people who personally doesn't click on the adverts, however I can assure you that your customers do.

Literally thousands of potential customers are clicking on those adverts everyday so don't be fooled by the urban myth. If you need further convincing, let me ask you this: How do you think Google has become a hugely profitable, multibillion dollar company? Nearly all of their revenue comes from Adwords (i.e. people clicking on the adverts!). So if you don't believe me when I say that people click on the adverts, then believe Google's profits!

One of the reasons Google is so successful is due to the fact that practically everyone uses it to search for what they need and so the amount of adverts they can serve to eager customers is staggering.

Google has one big advantage that makes it so incredibly powerful. It's the very fact that they display adverts based upon what someone is searching for.
If I type "new washing machine" into Google, then it's pretty clear that I'm in the market for a new washing machine, so any adverts that I see that match my needs are likely to get my attention (and probably my business!).

It's this targeting the right person at the right time and only paying if that person comes to my website that makes Google Adwords such a compelling solution for many businesses.

If Google Adwords is so great, why are there so many stories about businesses that have failed dramatically to make it work? Maybe you know one of these businesses. Maybe you are one of those businesses!

In reality, Adwords does work and I've seen it work very well for many businesses in many different types of industry. I've seen it work for different business models including business-to-customer ecommerce websites as well as business-to-business lead generation websites.

The reason it fails can usually be tracked down to a few basic mistakes. Basic but deadly!

Here are the big ones you should avoid.

Mistake 1: Picking The Wrong Keywords

As I've already said, adverts will appear on Google based upon what someone is typing into Google.

To do this, advertisers will pick the words that will trigger their adverts to appear. These are known as their keywords.

The mistake is simply that many businesses pick the wrong keywords. They usually pick a small number of the most obvious words. The problem is that all their competitors will do exactly the same thing and this means everyone is competing over the same small set of keywords. This generally means that the prices for clicks will be high for those adverts and frequently, it then becomes too expensive for many businesses. You've probably heard the complaint that "Adwords is too expensive". This is another myth. There are lots of keywords that are affordable for many businesses. It's just that everyone chases the popular and more expensive ones.

With proper keyword research, you can usually find a lot of excellent keywords that will drive highly qualified buyers to your website. Each of these keywords will not have anywhere near as many searches on Google as the popular ones that everyone else bids on, but when you've researched a sizable list of them, you will find yourself attracting a lot of customers successfully and all with reasonably priced clicks.

Mistake 2: One Advert Fits All

Quite often, businesses will write one advert and use it for all their Adwords advertising. This is a huge mistake.

If you recall, earlier I said that one of the big advantages of Adwords is that you can show your adverts to someone at the precise time they are looking on Google for a solution to their problem.

Since you will have a lot of keywords (or you should, if you read the section above!), then wouldn't it make sense to write adverts that are related specifically to groups of your keywords? The more directly related your advert is to what someone is typing into Google, then the more likely it is that they are going to click on your advert.

Here's an example of what I mean. Let's assume you own an online shoe shop. Let's say you sell shoes for men, women and children. It's likely then that you will have keywords for men's shoes, women's shoes and children's shoes. In that case, the advert for the men's shoes keywords should talk about men's shoes. The same is true for the keywords for women's shoes and children's shoes.

It's this grouping of keywords to specifically written adverts that is at the heart of successful Adwords advertising.

Mistake 3: Sending The Click To The Wrong Place

The internet is instant. It's changed our shopping habits completely. We are no longer content to browse around looking for what we want. We expect it to be served up to us, instantly.

So, if you've gone to all the hard work of writing an advert that's very specifically related to a set of keywords that relate to a particular product on your website - why would you NOT send them to the page for that product?

Unfortunately, I see businesses make this mistake all the time. Quite often, the adverts will all point to the website's home page. The visitors are then expected to find what they want by searching through the website or using the menu on the home page. They won't do this. They will hit the back button and choose someone else's advert.

So, make sure your adverts take people to the right page on your website. For example, if the advert is for red shoes, then send them to the page about red shoes. It's that simple.

One extra point to consider. If you've found some keywords that are perfect for your business and you don't have a really good page on your website that's specific to those keywords, then write one!

Mistake 4: Not Tracking Success

If I asked you to cross a road wearing a blindfold, then you'd tell me I was crazy.

You would be right but I see business owners who spend money on advertising without having any idea of how to measure if it's successful. They are literally crossing the road blindfolded!

Google Adwords has a free tracking service that will tell you which keywords and adverts are driving profitable traffic to your website.

It's called Conversion Tracking and it can be used to track which clicks successfully generate sales on your website. Even if your website isn't about making a sale but is actually about generating leads, then you can use Conversion Tracking to track if someone contacts you through the website. For example, it will track if they fill out your "contact us" form or your "call me back" form.

As I've already said, this service is free so there really is no reason not to use it. Also it's very simple to add to your website. You simply place some code onto the final success page. This page is usually referred to as the "thank you" page because it's the page that's displayed after someone has completed an action you want them to take on your website, such as "made a purchase" or filled out your contact form. The page usually says "*thank you for your purchase*" or "*thank you for filling out our form*" and that's why it's called a thank you page.

Of course, not only will Conversion Tracking tell you which keywords and adverts are successfully driving profitable sales or successful lead generation on your website, it will also tell you which ones aren't!

Now you have control. You can spend more on what's working and you can take action with the keywords and adverts that are not working.

Mistake 5: Not Scheduling Your Advertising

Are buyers looking for you 24 hours a day, every day?

Probably not and if they are, I guarantee there are times of the day (or days of the week) when they are more likely to buy from you than others.

With Adwords you can schedule when your adverts appear. This is a feature that is overlooked by many businesses and consequently they are running advertising at times when it is very unprofitable for them to do so.

Using Conversion Tracking (see point 4 above) allows you to see when you are getting conversions. You can see what hours of the day work best for you and also what days of the week. With this information, you can schedule your adverts to only run at the best times for your business. This can cut your advertising budget dramatically as you no longer run adverts at unprofitable times.

By the way, it's always worth testing different times and days rather than assuming that you know when you will be profitable. For example, if you are in the business to business market and you think your prospects will only be looking for you during office hours in the week, you may be surprised when you test this. I know of companies who run advertising over the weekend and drive people to a call back request form. On Monday mornings they usually have a number of these forms filled in and they start their week contacting these prospects. So you may find your prospects are looking for you during their downtime at the weekend because they are just too busy during their working week. Test it!

How To Be Very Sneaky With Advert Scheduling

There is another way that you can use advert scheduling to your advantage. You can write specific adverts for specific times.

Here's an example of what I mean.

Let's say you run a recruitment agency and you want to target people looking to change their current job. You could set up a campaign in Adwords that only runs on Mondays. The wording the adverts could say something like this;

"Monday Again. Can you face another week in your current job? We've loads of exciting jobs".

That would certainly get the attention of someone with Monday morning blues!

Of course, you could equally run another campaign that only showed adverts on a Friday and that could use an equally subtle approach.

"Thank God it's Friday. Do you want another week like that? Find a New, Exciting Job Today"

Mistake 6: Set It And Forget It

Whenever I am asked to look at a failing Adwords account, one of the things I often see is that they are still running the same adverts that they started with some months (even years!) before.

The key to success with Adwords is to constantly test and refine your advertising.

I guarantee that the first adverts you write will not be your best. They can be improved on and as you improve them, your sales and profits will improve. If you do not continually improve your advertising, then it will stagnate and suffer.

Luckily, Adwords provides you with the ability to test your adverts very easily. Rather than just running one advert for a set of keywords, you can run two adverts side by side to see which one generates the most profitable traffic for your website. You can then stop the least profitable advert and write yet another one to test against your current best advert.

Over time, this continual testing and refining of your adverts will increase your profitability.
In some cases, an Adwords account might start off as unprofitable but with this process of continually testing

and refining, I've seen those accounts turned around and become very profitable.

Lots of business will give up too early as their first sets of adverts don't instantly generate profits. They miss out on the pot of gold at the end of the rainbow, simply because they didn't test new ideas

By the way, once you've found adverts that work really well in Adwords, there is no reason why you can't take those adverts and use them in more traditional advertising. At least you know they work and you might find that your other advertising suddenly gets a boost from using proven adverts from Adwords.

Congratulations. You're On Your Way To Adwords Success

As I said at the beginning of this chapter, most people fail at Adwords because of these simple but avoidable mistakes.

Now that you know about them, you can avoid them and you'll be amazed at how successful you can be advertising with Adwords. Oh, and you'll be amazed at how big a smile it will put on your face!

About Mike Seddon

Mike Seddon is an online advertising specialist and author of the book Simply Adwords. His company, Internet Jetstream, helps businesses to harness the power of the internet and flood their website with a steady stream of buying customers. You can learn more about what Mike can do for you at **InternetJetstream.com** and you can also download your free copy of his Business Owners Guide to Google Adwords

CHAPTER 8

Good News

Donnie Bryant

I promise the details of this story are 100% true.

I ran into a beautiful woman I used to work with the other day. We engaged in the typical small talk for a few minutes, then the conversation turned to the projects we're working on these days. When I started talking about my projects, she smiled with her eyes and put her hand on my arm just above the elbow.

Know what my instant internal reaction was? *"Crap! My biceps are puny. This lady has probably lost all respect for me; she must think I'm a wimp. Why did I stop doing push ups?"*

The second thought that came to my mind was more than a little strange. I'll tell you about that in a minute. You can learn a lot about generating leads from my mini-muscles.

A Problem Is A Good Thing

When presented with a positive (attention from a member of the opposite sex) and a negative (my apprehension about looking weak to a member of the opposite sex), my mind fixated on the problem.

Guess what: *your prospective clients' brains work just like mine.* In most cases, the presence of or potential for a problem is more likely to win attention than the promise of benefits.

Problems Get Attention. Solving Them Gets Clients

Problems propel us through life and drive us to take action. They are the strongest selling force on earth.

As such, problems provide open doors into the lives of your prospective clients. Talking about the problems that gnaw at your prospects is a great way to generate targeted leads.

Entrepreneurs and marketers often get this wrong. You love your product, service and business, and rightly so. They are awesome, after all.

But You Can't Start Your Message There

The truth is that *nobody cares about your product - except you (and maybe your employees). Your* interests don't matter to clients. They have problems they want to get rid of and dreams they want to make into reality. *That* is what they care about. *That* is what they're thinking about.

If your product or service doesn't fix their problems and if your marketing doesn't address those problems, they won't care, no matter what benefits you promise.

Selling the benefits of your product can sabotage your lead generation efforts - if they are more important to you than the problems your ideal client is experiencing.

Look At It This Way

Every business exists to solve a problem. Restaurants feed hungry people. Plumbers fix clogged toilets. Movie theaters eliminate boredom.

Yet, just about every marketing training and resource out there tells you to focus on the benefits of your product or service.

The more you highlight a painful problem in your marketing messages, the more likely you are to strike a chord with the person suffering from that problem. You're more in touch with *his* feelings than *your* product. An out-of-reach dream is a problem.

A desire not yet satisfied is a problem.

"*I have a little bit of (fill in the blank), but I need* more" is a problem.

Being a problem-solver transforms you from a self-interested peddler into a helpful advisor.

Why Good News Isn't So Good

When you ask someone, "Do you want the good news or bad news?" the bad will command more attention every time.

From the client's perspective, leading with "good news" often sounds suspicious coming from somebody who is selling something:

- "You don't know me. How could you possibly know what's good news for me when you know nothing about me?"
- "I don't know you. Why should I trust you? You haven't proven yourself to me."
- "I bet this is good news *for you*. You obviously have a financial stake in this, so I'm inclined to believe you intend to *help yourself* by making sale *rather than to help me* by helping me fix my problem."
- "My life is fine. I'm not looking for solutions. Your good news doesn't excite me."

On the other hand, *people are always on the lookout for trouble*. When we catch a whiff of danger, we give it our full attention. That's how we protect ourselves and our loved ones from harm.

People also tend to personalize bad news automatically. When potential problems arise, they can't help but consider the personal ramifications. How will this affect me? They put up their guards to make sure they keep themselves safe. That often entails the active search for solutions (which you'd be happy to help them find).

It can be difficult for you, however, to personalize good news without making it sound like empty hype. If a potential client can't see the personal implications of your marketing message, you will have a difficult time getting him to take action.

Bad news creates room for the good news. Maybe more to the point, the *bad news is what makes the good news good*.

For example, when you feel healthy, medicine doesn't appeal to you at all. But when you start seeing signs of sickness in your body, you don't waste any time looking for a remedy.

So, Donnie Has No Muscles

Remember the situation I began this chapter with? When my lovely ex-coworker touched my arm, two thoughts entered my mind. The first, as you recall, was that my biceps weren't impressive enough.

The second thing I thought about was a series of Charles Atlas comic book ads from the 1940s.

Charles Atlas was a celebrity in his day, but his advertisements have made him an enduring legend and cultural icon. They are also among history's most famous lead generation materials.

If you're not familiar with advertisements, your favorite search engine can fix that in seconds. In short, the ads depict a scrawny guy being embarrassed in front of his girlfriend by a bigger, more muscular guy. The skinny guy gets mad, sends off for Charles Atlas' free bodybuilding booklet, quickly bulks up and goes back to even the score with the bully. "What a man!" the on-looking ladies would say. "And he used to be so skinny."

Take a look at these headline/titles:

- *"Hey, Skinny! Yer Ribs Are Showing!"*
- *The Insult that Made a Man out of Mac*
- *The Insult that Turned a 'Chump' Into a Champ*
- *How Jack the Weakling Slaughtered the Dance-Floor Hog*

Each headline tells a story that begins with a problem. Readers who felt the pain of being skinny, weak or insulted were helplessly curious to know what happened. The problem grabbed their attention, pulling them into the story. As the narrative progressed, the solution emerged. That's when Atlas offered a free sample of his problem-solving solution, that booklet that made a man out of Mac. Thousands of guys who wanted to become stronger sent in their contact information and became high-quality leads.

Forbes Magazine selected Charles Atlas as one of the 20th Century's Super Salesmen based largely on the strength and effectiveness of this approach to marketing. You can use the same principles to become a super salesman of your products and services.

Generating Leads through Problem-Solving: Your Action Plan

Concentrating on problems and pains isn't the only way to get people's attention. It is my preferred method and the one I nearly always prescribe for my clients. Problems simply have greater psychological and emotional impact than benefits. Study after study shows that fear of loss is more powerful than desire for gain. That's just how our brains are wired.

Talking about problems is the surest way I know of to gain attention. News media knows it and does it. Water-cooler gossip proves it out.

Committing to becoming a problem-solver is a foundational mindset that should become the springboard for your lead generation campaigns.

Review your current marketing. Is it *product-pitching* or *problem-focused*?

Product-pitching → Self-centered

Problem-solving → Client-centered

1. Re-orient your marketing materials to *isolate* and address the pressing issues your ideal clients are facing right now. Talking about the bad news gets those prospects to identify themselves. They want to know more about what you have to say and what you can do for them.

2. Work on becoming a trustworthy source of information on the problem you fix. When you *educate* your potential clients about their problem, you also teach them how to make decisions on buying goods and services in your industry. That gives you a distinct advantage over everyone else in your space.

Whose input do *you* want guiding their buying choices?

3. Offer a solution to *alleviate* the problem.

The more *specifically-tailored* the offer is to the prospect, the better. For example, if you sell a book of remedies for back pain, you may create a version of the book for women in their 40s who suffer from lower back pain originating from childbearing.

The more you zero in on the particular issue, the more valuable the information is perceived to be. It's easier for the client to believe it will speak directly to them and help them personally. There's less fear of disappointment.

Will you lose a portion of your audience? Probably. But your offer will be far more compelling to the people who you're trying to help.

Plus, it gives you the opportunity to make several specialized niche offerings instead of just a general one.

Create a free or low-cost way for potential clients to get this information in exchange for contact information. It could be digital (report, video, MP3, email mini-series, webinar), physical (book, CD, DVD, newsletter) or personal (phone consultation). Make it as valuable as you can. *Just because it's free doesn't mean you don't have to sell it!*

Then, you have to put your offer where the right eyes will see it.

Going Forward

This may be a major change from the way you usually approach marketing. Up until now, you may have been unintentionally self-centered, focusing too much on yourself and the needs of your business when you should have been concentrating on solving problems for the people who make up your client base.

Today is the day that changes.

About Donnie Bryant

Donnie Bryant is a direct response copywriter and marketing consultant. He helps small businesses and solo professionals connect with and convert their "should-be" clients with unusually effective marketing messages and systems. Find out more about Donnie at **http://donnie-bryant.com.**

If you're interested in learning more about connecting with your "should-be" clients, you can download Donnie's free report "Hard-to-Resist Lead Generation Offers" at **http://donnie-bryant.com/htrleadgen.**

CHAPTER 9

Using NeuroLinguistic Programming (NLP) To Draw In Rabidly-Hungry, Highly Qualified Leads

Jonathan Altfeld

Many entrepreneurs today are at least aware of NLP, if not trained in it.

After all, NLP is completely focused on the structure of subjectivity, and on influencing minds to have more choice, make better decisions, and change perspectives. Every entrepreneur and marketer needs to be good at

these things. There is a natural fit between the two domains of expertise of marketing and NLP.
NLP Practitioners and Trainers ought to study marketing, to better sell their services and manage their business. Marketers benefit from using NLP, to become better at structuring the language of their offers, and for other reasons. However, don't assume that because these fields contribute so much to each other, that one set of skills is identical to the other. They really aren't similar. They simply *inform* each other in valuable ways.

This chapter aims to help you use aspects of NLP to get more leads and more profitable customers.

To do this we look at (1) your goals, (2) your own emotional state management, (3) how well you pace and lead other people's experiences, (4) how effectively you elicit emotional investment and initiate action from other people, and (5) how you structure the language of your lead generation campaigns to maximize responses.

No matter how good you are at most of these five areas, if you falter in any one of the above areas, your lead generation process could fail on a grand scale.

NLP helps enormously in each of these five areas. Keeping in mind that books are a poor substitute for live training, hopefully this chapter will do a good job of providing you immediately actionable ideas to help you improve in these five areas.

Finally, here's a hint: You would benefit from doing the exercises in at least the next two sections before reading and using the ideas throughout the rest of this book. Setting great outcomes, and managing your state, can make all the difference in the world between someone who never takes action, and someone who takes their learning really seriously, gets incredibly excited by the possibilities of trying out what these amazing experts suggest you do, and then takes massive action to build empires.

"Well Formed Outcomes" To Ensure You're Taking Action Towards Truly Achievable Goals

There is a reason that most personal development professionals begin their books and DVDs and seminars with a section on setting goals or outcomes. If you don't know where you're going, how will you know if you've gotten there?

In NLP we prefer the distinction of choosing "outcomes" as opposed to setting "goals."

Goals are some distant future line or endpoint. Outcomes are the eventual result of some specific course of action. Goals involve a future orientation, when viewed from the present, looking just at possibilities. Outcomes involve a past orientation, when viewed from the future beyond the outcome, looking backward through time at "done deals."

This distinction is more than just semantic; it involves a different neurology and orientation for each of us. Choosing outcomes allows us to take advantage of a wonderful time distortion effect, to make more vivid the potential paths between the current moment, and the outcome we want to build. The more vividly we imagine them, the easier it is to take those steps, and the more comfortable we'll be, when we do take those steps.

So don't set goals; instead choose outcomes.

In NLP, there are a few principles we apply to choosing outcomes, that help us maximize the likelihood of success. We call these the "Well-Formedness Principles of Outcomes."

1. No Nots. Don't use negation. Have you ever told a child "Don't drop that!" What happens? Solutions should not be designed while mired in

our problem states. Phrase your outcomes exclusively in the positive. Don't talk about what you don't want to happen anymore. Describe what specifically you want to positively create/achieve/cause. Don't talk about turning around a poor lead generation problem. Talk about building a flood of quality leads. Pick an outcome of filling your downline with as much as or maybe even slightly more than you're set up to serve, if a high percentage of those leads converted.

2. Your outcomes should be reasonable for the timeframe you allow. Depending on your niche, taking over your entire market completely may be a lofty outcome, but it's probably not reasonable. If a reasonable yet still desirable first outcome is grabbing 10% or 20% of your market share, set that as a first outcome. That may be very reasonable. Some have been known to echo “there are no unreasonable outcomes, just unreasonable timeframes!”
3. You should be able to initiate movement and maintain progress towards this outcome yourself with minimal dependencies. In the case of online advertising, this means writing or at least approving your own ads, and managing the day

to day expenditures and demographics of that advertising, yourself.

4. You should be able to test for progress and milestones towards your desired outcome, using (ideally) your five senses. If you're relying on interpretations that you cannot control, that may not be well-formed. As this applies to lead-generation, make sure you're using quality metrics for your advertising and quality data analysis for your overall marketing funnel.

Ensuring your desired stated outcomes match these principles doesn't guarantee easy results, but does maximize the likelihood of getting the results you want. So don't skip this step - for any endeavor, always begin by setting desired outcomes and ensuring they match these principles!

"State Management" For Self (The Contagion Of Passion And Confidence)

If you want to succeed, Passion and Confidence are among the two most powerful emotions to find inside yourself, and learn to amplify them. There are many other useful and contagious emotions to be explored for lead-generation purposes, but let's discuss these two as amongst your most important inner resources.

Most people make decisions emotionally. Most decisions are not rational.

Facts are important. And specific factual statistics can also significantly increase buy-in.

However, **people will still always make their decisions emotionally**, and then use facts to help justify the decisions they've already made, emotionally.
Now, consider that all emotions are, to some degree or other, contagious. That contagion affects people the most, in person, but it also affects people on the phone, or from a stage, or through video, through audio, or even print or online ads. If you are feeling doubtful about a particular phrasing, your customer may feel doubtful about your product. Emotions are contagious and often become too broad a brush in the hands of our customers. We need to take charge of our emotional states.

All emotions are a carrier wave for your message, and are often the most influential part of your message. I invite you to dig deep inside yourself and nurture an inner well of passion and confidence that you can amplify, feel deeply, and operate from. These two emotions will infuse and inform everything you say and do.

You can't afford to be blasé about or disinterested in your product or service. You can't afford to be uncertain or doubtful about your product or service. If there are faults in the product or service or offering that would threaten the strength or integrity of your passion or confidence, get those things fixed ASAP.

In the next section, we'll describe and discuss Pacing and Leading. You will be leading people to new perspectives, when you request their lead-qualifying actions. And you will never be able to effectively lead people from your own states of doubt, boredom, uncertainty, worry, etc. These less useful emotions will leak into all of your marketing efforts.

So how can you elicit passion and confidence inside yourself? We call this re-vivifying a state. There are a range of techniques in NLP to help with this, including "the Circle of Excellence." Here is an oversimplified version in brief:

Think about the most passionate reason why (a) you're in business, or (b) about your product or service, or (c) what you hope to accomplish for yourself and others through your product or service, or (d) what you hope to accomplish for yourself and others after making it big through this and other products and services. Or, go back to a time or place when and/or where you felt intense Passion about something. See what you saw then, hear what you heard then, feel what you felt then. Go back through these different sights, sounds, feelings, rotate through these sense-memories, until the feeling amplifies inside you.

If you're still not getting a result, have someone else lead you through this, from a state of passionate confidence. (Not from a state of confusion or doubt, because emotions are contagious, remember?)

You'll notice that the more often and frequently you do the above, the faster these states become available to you by choice, when you need them. NLP has other techniques to speed that access up; one of the best is called Anchoring. Please take my word for it that you cannot learn anchoring well from a book (or from most trainers, in my opinion - it's a very nuanced skill).

Do this process to find passion. Then do this to find confidence. Then, when you sit down to make progress on your lead generation, make sure you're feeling passion and confidence and can fire them up at will.

There are other useful states to find and manage, for lead generation purposes. One great emotion is a sense of managed risk. There is uncertainty in risk, but not necessarily doubt.

I believe you gain immensely by becoming skilled at managing risk. Entrepreneurs make mistakes, and they also measure and test alternatives. They experiment a lot. If you're operating out of fear, you likely won't experiment enough to find out what works for you and your marketplace. You need to shed that fear, and learn to manage risk.

Managing risk involves a sense of adventure, and a desire for knowledge. The mindset and emotions of people who manage risk well are unrelated to blind gambling. Entrepreneurs use a form of very conscious gambling, but they rarely gamble with 'the whole game.' They think systemically, but with flexibility, constantly refining and varying their systems as they learn new knowledge.

They rarely put all their eggs in one basket. They look at options, they evaluate the likelihood of success for multiple options, and they make a measured guess based on what they know, in terms of which choices are risks most worth taking. And to measure that, they'll always choose levels of investment that they're willing to risk, while looking for the best result possible, knowing that not everything will pan out. When they choose a specific risk and it doesn't pan out, the loss of that investment is not seen as a loss, its seen as a valuable lesson.

Over time, learning to manage risk well leaves a trail of enough highly successful results, that those can then be scaled higher up. Managing risk and then scaling up the most successful approaches, is an incredibly smart move.

Embrace taking smart risks. Manage them at a small level. Accept and learn from losses, collect and learn from wins, and then, as successful results emerge, scale up. Risk small, repeatedly, then later, win big.

Managing risks often involves a somewhat playful emotion. Playful curiosity and anticipation.

So the above are a few highly useful emotions you want to develop and nurture.

What if you're stuck in less useful emotions, such as worry, or doubt, or low confidence, or anger, or fear? This could be killing your marketing or lead-generation results in ways you'd have a lot of trouble quantifying. And you may never see how it happens.

If you're feeling these unwanted emotions enough to pollute your performance and results, you definitely need some form of state interrupt. Here are several ways to get out of bad states:

- **Touch your tongue to the roof of your mouth** - it kills the internal dialogue that may have kept you asking awful questions of yourself, which in turn kept you cycling through bad feelings.
- **It's much harder to turn an emotion down, than to turn it up!** Instead of trying not to feel fear, feel enough fear about something that you get angry, and then get angry enough to laugh about it. Feelings turn up much more quickly than they diminish, and they're surprisingly easy to redirect as they amplify.
- **The fastest way to change your state, is to change your posture and/or breathing rate.** This will always be true! Get up! Go take a walk! Do some yoga! Get on a treadmill or bike! Do jumping jacks! You'd be shocked how well this works to change your state. Our knowledge on this over the past 40 years was recently validated by Harvard Business Professor Amy Cuddy. She studied Power Postures, and found that if you stand in a victory posture for two minutes, you

will start feeling more powerful and confident. Act as if... and you become so.

So to get the maximum possible out of this topic, imagine a time in the future, perhaps several, where you might catch yourself in some unresourceful state... and plan, now, during the exercise, to become aware then, in the future... of that less than useful state. Then imagine yourself doing one or some of the above suggestions to help you pop back into a more resourceful emotion, like passion, and/or confidence! See what you'd see after becoming more resourceful. Hear what you'd hear, and feel what you'd feel. Play the movies out in your mind to their logical better conclusions. This will help immensely!

"Pacing And Leading" To Keep People's Attention For The Right Reasons, And Become More Gently Persuasive While Still Validating Others' Perspectives

The concepts of pacing and leading are central to all studies of Rapport. NLP techniques work best when they are sandwiched between efforts to build and maintain rapport. And when we're generating quality leads, we do want rapport with our market, and with our audiences. We want them to feel in rapport with us.

We want them to feel like we get them. We understand them. They, in turn, will always prefer to feel that we know their hopes, dreams, pain, discomfort, challenges, goals, values, and beliefs.

This idea of pacing and leading implies that we begin by matching someone's reality in some way.

If you don't know what pacing refers to, perhaps you've seen pace cars in Auto Racing, where one car will drive the pace of the pack for one pass along the track. Or perhaps you've seen footage of the Tour de France bicycle race. You may have seen bicycle team members pace each other (when followers draft very closely behind a lead cyclist). By keeping pace with another person, we're showing them that we know where they are.

Pacing and leading, in general, can be done nonverbally, verbally and visually. For our purposes here, I'm primarily referring to visual or verbal contexts. Our messages need to cause people to feel like we get them. We know where they are and what they're facing. We understand their lives.

What Makes Pacing And Leading So important?

People are unlikely to accept our influence - our leading statements or questions - unless they first feel paced.

You may have heard of the catch-phrase “People don't care how much you know until they know how much you care.” This applies in lead-generation as much as it does anywhere else.

Joe Prospect doesn't want your emails unless you know and can quickly express something about the challenges he personally faces.

Jane Prospect doesn't want to know about your seminars or receive mail about them, unless those seminars speak directly to what they're aiming to accomplish right now.

Fred Prospect does not want any of your phone calls encouraging him to buy your latest family planning home study course if Fred is a single unattached guy.

You need to effectively pace, before you'll be allowed or invited to lead (and expect people to follow).

Headlines in particular work beautifully when they both pace and lead people in the most succinct and vibrant way possible.

"State Elicitation" In Others (Curiosity, Hunger, Desire, Deprivation, Envy, Etc.)

Understand that when you first contact another potential lead through whatever means, at the moment they're exposed to your ad or message, few if any of them are feeling the emotions they would need to feel, in order to buy in. And few are feeling enough of what they'd need to feel, to spend more than a few seconds on your message.

In our information-rich, social-media-driven world, your message probably interrupts people in some way. In fact, we might even say... it needs to.

In NLP, we call this a "pattern interrupt", and typically, after something interrupts our attention, all of us will give that stimulus a widely varying 2-10 second opportunity, to capture and lead our attention. Only then, if our attention was sufficiently captivated, would we decide to spend more time reading, viewing, or listening to your message.

Your message needs to rapidly elicit some form of desire or curiosity. Curiosity is an amazing emotion, and it is essential that you learn how to better create or cause other people to become curious. It's a very *flexible* emotion. If you get someone curious, they'll give you tacit permission to lead them almost anywhere interesting. Think... “I'm curious about...” and you realize that this sentence fragment could lead anywhere.

Here are some great ways to generate Curiosity or Fascination, or even a deep need to know more:

- **Pacing & Leading** (as we already discussed). Pace the problem they're facing from their perspective, inside their world, then elegantly lead them to want to know about your solution. If you can effectively describe what its like to have that problem and to feel it now, then you've paced them. They feel well understood, and they're more likely to hear out your efforts to influence.
- **Induce new pain** - find their pain points and amplify them to logical extremes, then mention secondary consequences they may not even have considered, as the current problem snowballs and leads to others. Do this through stories or metaphors, and then: **provide a relief valve of some kind,** and associate that relief valve with

your product or service (or with signing up for more information).

- **Teasers and Loss Leaders** - you can do this by hinting about the value someone's going to get AFTER they take some first active step (like giving you an email address, and/or a name, phone number, emails of friends and family, whichever).
- **Cliff-hangers** - this is the big brother to teasers. The one best cliff-hanger I've ever experienced, that saved hundreds of lives, and prevented losses by the million$, is
- **Describe, physically, what curiosity feels like**, without ever mentioning the word curious, or curiosity, etc. *"You know that odd and wonderful sensation you sometimes get where you know an aha moment is coming? For some its like a tingling in the temples, or in the neck... a sense of a smile waiting in the wings... a warm anticipation of discovery...."* This is usually less effective than precisely pacing someone's own current problem state, and providing the hint of a great solution, but it can work a charm!

Experiment with these. You will find that virtually everyone who shares their information with you for the purposes of learning more about you (and thus, pre-qualifying themselves to you as a lead) is feeling something like curiosity at that moment. Don't get lost in the minutia: Your job, specifically during lead generation, is to induce relief from pain, and/or utter curiosity, through the act of qualifying themselves to you.

Each of these two (both pain, and curiosity) works well. **Do both together, and your lead generation will accelerate rapidly.** In NLP we call this a **Propulsion System**. If you attend live NLP training, make sure your trainer knows how to both explain propulsion systems, and demonstrate them not only linguistically, but also spatially.

"Structuring The Language Of Your Lead Generation Campaigns To Maximize Responses"

If I ask you what type of businesses you run, and what your biggest job is, you're likely to give me any of a million different answers. Ultimately, as an entrepreneur, you have just one job. To be effective at sharing and spreading a message. To do this well, you either have to be an absolute natural at creating specific perceptions in people's minds very quickly, or... you have to *learn* to do it well.

This is where NLP shines like crazy.

There, I just used NLP within this chapter. I said NLP shines like crazy. Shining is a visual word. It's a sensory rich word. When I use the metaphor of shining to describe NLP, it doesn't take you more than a few microseconds to make sense of it.

I didn't say, "Here is where learning NLP will be most beneficial." That sentence, by contrast to NLP shining like crazy, uses an unspecific verb, "learning," that takes a lot more time to unpack and represent, in our minds.

Now listen to and feel the difference between the phrase "feel the love" and "loving yourself". One involves an unspecified noun (Love), the other, an activity that likely involves movies in our minds. Some will never learn the difference, but one is helpful to our marketing, the other slows it down.

Sensory-unspecified nouns and process verbs (as opposed to active sensory rich verbs) will slow down your message uptake in prospects' minds. This will dramatically lower your conversion rates.

If you want to **kick-start** your campaigns with the greatest chance of **hitting the jackpot**, then **shine a light** on how you **choose words** and how you **fill** your prospects **ears** with ideas and solutions that'll be a **perfect fit** for their needs.

Sensory rich language doesn't slow us down, and we can still agree or disagree with what we hear, but we do so more quickly. And the more quickly a good prospect agrees with your writing, the less your writing slows them down, confuses them, the better.

So Where Best To Begin Applying NLP To Lead Generation?

I strongly recommend you begin with the first two sections of this chapter, and get really good at choosing Outcomes, and then at Pacing and Leading. Then, among the others, work on your weakest area the most. Because that's where you'll see the best results for your efforts.

All performance modeling in NLP operates from having a great example to follow (and sometimes that's just imagined clearly in our minds. And then we look at what we're currently getting. We get our best results by always focusing on what needs the most attention; where are we weakest at the moment? And when we get good enough at that area, such that another area becomes the most obvious weak link, then we're ready to work on another area.

I wish you only the best possible results - and my final recommendation is, develop consistency, be systematic, but keep varying your systems. Persistent, systematic flexibility will get you there!

About Jonathan Altfeld

Jonathan Altfeld's background included 2 years in Cornell Architecture School, and then he finished his undergraduate degree with an interdisciplinary focus on Computer Science, Philosophy, and Literature. He's had two careers, a first in Artificial Intelligence software (he's published), and a second, in NLP Training (and he's run courses all over the globe for nearly two decades).

Jonathan is a guitarist, pianist, and drummer; he plays didgeridoo, and can sing. He enjoys tennis, bicycling, and skiing. He makes an amazing channa masala, and loves raw green juice. He can draw, paint, and sculpt, and as a gifted graphologist and personality type expert, he can tell you more about you in a brief meeting or by reading your handwriting, than most of your friends or colleagues know!

And in spite of all that, he's still working on getting his kids to listen.

For our readers, as of 2015, Jonathan brings 18 years of experience using NLP to help entrepreneurs just like you to get better results, anywhere in your lives. Whether improving your lead generation results, or through solving problems, designing in-house courses, improving your sales systems, smoothing challenging relationships, or coaching you to read people and then communicate more effectively, Jonathan's coaching and consulting is always an investment with rapid and high ROI, never a cost. His best result to date was to help one of his regular sales coaching clients to reclaim a lost $180,000 sale, during just 15 minutes of coaching.

Would You Like to Take Advantage of Jonathan's Offer?

Grab your copies of Jonathan Altfeld's **Introductory CD** and the world's most thorough **sensory-rich vocabulary list**, as well as explore Jonathan's other offerings, here:

http://www.altfeld.com/leadgen

Jonathan works with companies, executives, and other high-performers looking to step up to higher levels. He focuses mostly on business applications of NLP, offering seminars, home-study resources, a blog, and extensive articles. He coaches and consults on communication and training, marketing, website copy, launch funnels, and more.

http://www.altfeld.com/leadgen

CHAPTER 10

Will Your Landing Page Turn Visitors Into Customers? How To Quickly Tell

Bnonn Tennant

Any kind of marketing *just is* creating thought sequences your prospect ("Sam") goes through to move from awareness of your existence to taking action as a buyer.

This means that optimizing your marketing–including your landing pages, email autoresponders, sales pages, upsells and what-have-you–is actually a case of optimizing Sam's thought sequences.

Put another way, optimization doesn't take place *on your landing page.* It takes place *in Sam's mind.* So understanding how his mind works online, and how his brain naturally processes a web-page, can help you structure your content much more effectively.

Response rates increase dramatically when your page is designed to mimic Sam's natural thought sequence. And this thought sequence can be understood quite simply with a framework I call FRODO:

First Reaction (FR)

"How does this site make me feel?" The first question Sam asks–even if unconsciously. This is exactly like our first impression of people: an emotional snap judgment made in our limbic systems within 4/10s of a second. A positive first reaction will improve conversions; a negative one will push them down. The First Reaction is governed by how your site is "dressed":-

1. **Layout & Proportion**. Are the page's elements laid out in a familiar way that Sam can understand instantly without having to think: masthead at the top, navigation below, search on the top right, and body content aligned along the left margin? Is the layout open and inviting, or does a lack of whitespace make it seemed

cramped and hard to read? Are the major page elements proportioned to the Golden Ratio–for example, in a 2-column layout, is the body width about 62%, with a 38% sidebar? (See fig. 1 for an example of a well-proportioned and laid out page structure.)

2. **Typography.** Is the body copy set on a consistent vertical grid–just as music is set to a consistent rhythm? Is it presented using a consistent font with a "personality" appropriate to the site? (For example, an old book-style font will look incongruous on a tech startup's website, while a modern sans-serif will fit right in.) Is it set at a consistent size which has been chosen because it is easy to read, rather than because the web designer thought it looked good–at least 16 pixels? Are the lines no more than about 80 characters long, with a height between them around 140% of the font size? And are there plenty of scannable elements for Sam's eyes to fixate on, like drop caps, short paragraphs, subheads, and lists?

3. **Color.** Is the page designed with an attractive palette, featuring no more than four main colors? Is this palette appropriate for the site–does it match its personality? Is the body copy set black

on white (or close enough), so that it is highly legible; rather than reversed, which is extremely hard to read? Is color used to guide the eye in a logical path, or are some elements too visually dominant, standing out when they should not?

4. **Expectations.** Does the site match or exceed what Sam was expecting–or does it trigger feelings of uncertainty? For example, a B2B landing page often works better with navigation that links it to the larger business site, because Sam expects businesses to have large sites which reflect their structure and products. An orphaned page alone in the ether makes him uneasy. By the same token, if he arrived via an ad, the page should deliver exactly what the ad promised, with similar wording.

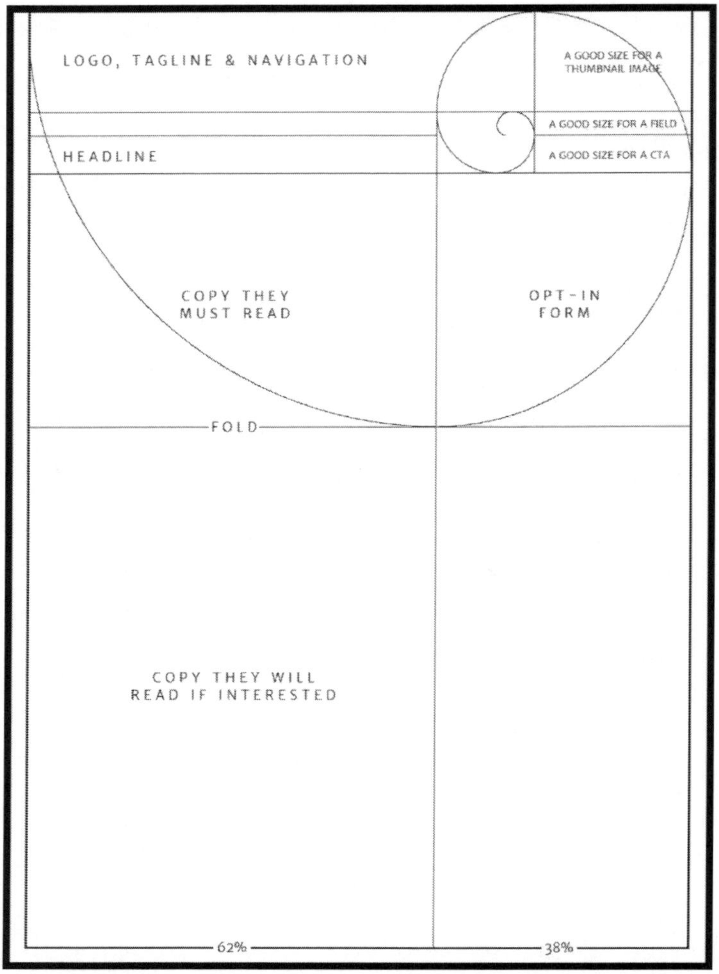

Figure 1, above: an example of a well-proportioned and laid-out page using the Golden Ratio.

Orientation (O)

"Am I in the right place?"–is the second question Sam asks. The page must look promising at first blush; if he doesn't feel confident about where he is within at most

7 seconds, he'll generally leave rather than trying to figure it out. Therefore, every page must clearly orient him. There are four places he looks for orienting information:-

1. **Masthead.** This includes both your logo and tagline. Even a self-explanatory logotype–such as "Jameson Web Design"–will benefit from a tagline to further explain the site's purpose. Make sure it actually does this, though–three adjectives separated by periods may look arty as hell, but it's utterly useless to Sam, who will tend to think you're a pretentious git. Use clear language Sam himself would use, and avoid "creative" slogans and jargon.

2. **Navigation.** This is the first place Sam glances to get a sense for the site's structure–the places he can go and the options available to him. Not all landing pages benefit from navigation, but many do so it's worth testing. Is the navigation clearly identifiable, with items labeled in a conventional way–or is it hard to spot, with "branded" labels Sam doesn't understand? (For example, "Carrier Pigeon" instead of "Contact"–Sam won't click on mystery meat links.)

3. **Search.** Over 50% of web users are search-oriented, so if you have navigation on your page it should include a search bar which is clearly identifiable–located on or next to the navigation element, at the top right of the page, with a button labeled "Search".

4. **Headline.** Your headline serves two key purposes; both of which make it the most important element on your page. It is the main element Sam looks for to understand, via keywords, what the specific page he is on is about; and it also compels him into the copy by implying the benefit or value of reading. In terms of orientation, Sam won't stick around if the headline suggests he is not where he wanted to be; so make sure its wording reiterates, expands on, or progresses the thought which was on his mind when he arrived. Put another way, the headline must closely match the call to action that directly preceded it, whether that was a PPC ad, an email link, a banner, or whatever.

Desirability (D)

"Will I gain more than I invest?" Sam always wonders this–if not in as many words–before he clicks on *anything*. So before you ask him to click you must explain the value. His perceived return must be greater than his perceived investment. This is always measured primarily in *emotion*–not in time or money.

If the investment is small the desirability can be small too. But if it is the potential emotional turmoil and effort of talking to someone, if it is the pain of parting with hard-earned cash, then the desirability must be high. There are four main factors which affect this:-

1. **Headline.** This has to make Sam read your copy; if it doesn't, you won't get any conversions. This is why the headline is the most important element on your page: it is what decides whether Sam will give you enough time to persuade him to convert. To do this, you must:

   - *Connect* with what he is already thinking. Take the question, problem, fear or desire already on his mind, and appeal to his self-interest there; then put yourself in his shoes, read the headline you've written and ask, "So what?" If you can't answer, rewrite.
   - *Contrast* your message with what he has heard before. Even if it is not new, it must *sound* new, or he will tend to dismiss it. Metaphors are useful here ("Melts fat like a furnace"), as are other kinds of word pictures,

especially combined with humor ("They'll fight over it when you're dead"). Sometimes, controversy, baffling statements, or even simple shock value can be effective too ("Read this or die").

- *Clearly* convey your message. If you're not using language Sam himself would use, you've already lost him. Pick simple words rather than complex ones; precise rather than vague or puffy ones; and concrete rather than abstract ones. You want Sam to be able to visualize what you're saying–even hear, smell, touch or taste it. The more real the better. This is surprisingly counterintuitive, because we want to show off in headlines. Resist the urge at all costs; your page is for Sam, not for you. Stamping down your ego is well worth it when you look at your conversion metrics.

2. **Body copy.** The purpose of your copy is to get Sam from what he believes about your offer when he arrives, to the belief that he should take you up on it immediately. Whether the page is a lead-generation form offering a free PDF, or a sales letter for your $90,000 flagship product, you can use the "Four Ps":-

- *Promise* him something;
- *Picture* that promise fulfilled;

- *Prove* that you can fulfill it;
- *Push* him to accept your offer.

Whatever you're asking Sam to do, don't focus on selling it. You're not an advocate for your *offering;* you're an advocate for *Sam.* Genuinely care that he makes the choice which is best for him. Then explain, in exactly the same way as if you were speaking directly to him, how you believe your offering *is* best for him. Clarity trumps persuasion. People hate being sold to and know when you're trying to do it. But they love to buy, and they love feeling they've been helped to make a wise decision. If you can make Sam feel that way, you'll do well.

3. **Images.** Images convey desirability with great force–*provided* they're used correctly. However, it may surprise you to learn that *most* images on the web are not used correctly, and actually *depress* conversions. Simply put, images must demonstrate to Sam that his return will outweigh his investment. In most cases copy does this better, which is why websites with flashy graphics or stock photos perform poorly. But there are times when images convey value more effectively than copy:-

   - Hero shots help Sam relate to the author as a real person;

- Very high quality product shots show rather than tell, so Sam can see what he gets–the closest he can come online to turning the product over in his hands, or walking around it in a showroom;
- Trends & statistics are easy to grasp when presented graphically.

4. **Speed.** The "faster" your page feels the better it will do. Long sign-up forms with numerous fields look like a lot of effort; they are slow. Multiple columns of text slow Sam down because he doesn't know which one to read first. Excess verbiage prevents him finding the information he wants, stalling his momentum. Conversely, "mad libs" forms, or multi-stage forms are quick; a single column of text keeps his eyes in the right place at all times; and clear subheads, bullets and calls to action help him rapidly get the gist of your value proposition as he scans down the page.

Offers (O)

"Do my goals match the available options?" Sam wonders, looking at the links and buttons at the end of the copy. Assuming the desirability elements have been done right, the final hurdle the page must overcome on the way to success is the offers, or calls to action (CTAs). How well these will work is determined by four factors:-

1. **Placement.** Is what is being offered the same thing that Sam wants *at this point on the page?* Is the offer logical given what he currently knows and feels–or is it asking for a commitment he's not yet ready to make? You must consider his goals and fit the page's objectives to these–forcing unnatural objectives on him, regardless of what he wants, is never effective. For example, very often I see business homepages with primary CTAs asking me to buy something. This is illogical–like asking a prospect to buy as soon as he walks in the door of your office.

   Note that whether a call to action falls above or below the fold is largely irrelevant; what matters is whether it falls in a logical place given the thought sequence Sam must go through. If you need a fair amount of copy to convert him, it will fall below the fold; if you need only a little, it may fall above.

2. **Visibility.** Does the call to action (especially the button) stand out? It is almost impossible to make a call to action button too large. As it gets bigger

it will get more clicks–but it must look clickable. Dimension is important here: giving the button a sense of standing out from the page. The more tactile you can make it (including mouse-over effects), the better. In terms of color, don't get caught up in endless research on who got what conversion rates with which button color–rather, start by finding the color that has the most contrast with everything else on the page.

3. **Phrasing.** Does the call to action copy reiterate the payoff Sam *gets* ("Get your free personality report"–or does it reiterate what he must *do* ("Click here to submit")? The former will always work better than the latter. Buttons should start with a verb like "Get", and essentially act as a second headline. If all Sam reads is your headline and call to action–not an improbable scenario–he should have a clear, forceful sense of why he should click. It is also a good idea to couch CTA copy in the first person–"Get my report" rather than "Get your report".

4. **Weight.** On pages with more than one objective, consider two calls to action which both reflect logical goals Sam may want to fulfil–and of course work towards the site's main objective. Offer graded levels of investment to create an

either/or rather than a yes/no decision, and ensure these buttons are visually distinct, with one having greater size, brightness, or some other kind of contrast to the other.

The ACE Principle For Designing And Arranging Page Elements

Attention = Contrast + Eyepath.

You can get a great deal right with the FRODO framework, but still produce an ineffective page by not following the ACE principle:-

Attention: An element needs to get attention if it is included on the page. If it *doesn't* get Sam's attention at *some* stage, then there's no point having it on the page at all. But the *time* at which it gets Sam's attention must be right. It's pointless for an offer to get his attention before he has read the copy which establishes its desirability. And it's pointless for the copy to get his attention before he knows where he is and whether he wants to read it. This is why the FRODO framework is listed in the order it is: each element must get attention in sequence. You don't optimize pages; you optimize thought sequences.

Contrast: This helps Sam to see at a glance which elements are the most important. Elements which reflect major items of concern, like orientation and offers, should have higher contrast. Text elements should also have varying contrast: the headline should stand out more than subheads or the logo; subheads more than body copy, and so on. Contrast is achieved in four basic ways:-

- *Color.* Bright colors, particularly red and orange, catch Sam's attention.
- *Dimension.* Larger elements, unusual shapes, or three-dimensional elements will stand out more.
- *Movement.* Animation gets a lot of attention and should generally be avoided; but implied movement (eg arrows) are very effective for catching Sam's eye and moving it in the direction you want it to go.
- *Separation.* Anything that stands alone, or is different (eg color, shape, whitespace) will catch Sam's eye.

Eyepath: In the West, Sam reads left to right, top to bottom. Elements must therefore fall logically into that path: orientation before desirability before offers. This eyepath *can* be strategically altered with the use of contrast, if it is important to do so–for example, a high-contrast lead-gen form on the right side of the page can get Sam's attention and investment before he spends time reading the main copy, which might see a high initial abandonment rate.

Better Page Response With FRODO And ACE

This is all the space I have to explain these principles here. But you might like to follow up with free training that goes deeper into optimizing your top 5 page elements. It includes clear, succinct "dos" and "don'ts", coupled with plenty of real life examples, and is completely based on scientific testing rather than opinion. To get this training, go here:

www.attentionthievery.com

About D Bnonn Tennant

Bnonn is a conversion optimization consultant, copywriter and web designer. As well as being the creator of the conversion coaching program "Attention-Thievery Academy", he has written dozens of articles on increasing response for industry blogs like Unbounce, Copyblogger, Smashing Magazine, Problogger and KISSmetrics. When he isn't elbow-deep in the guts of someone's landing page, he is bow-hunting, mountainbiking, or teaching his kids how to grapple a zombie without getting bit.

CHAPTER 11

Bridging The Gap Between Robot And Customer

Eugene Farber

How To Do SEO Like A Real-World Marketer And Get Google To Send You Business

"How would you like to get right in front of the people that are actively seeking to buy what you have to offer?"

That is precisely the question I ask when speaking to a potential client about the possibility of doing some SEO (search engine optimization) work for them.

It's hard to deny the power of search engines. They are ingrained in everyday life and they have an extraordinary power over where people spend their money.
Anecdotally, most people I know go straight for a search engine when they are looking for an answer or a source to buy from. But the stats support the anecdotal evidence.

A study from Forrester Research showed that 9 out of 10 purchasing decisions begin on the internet. Fleishman-Hillard's research shows that 89% of consumers turn to search engines to help them decide where to spend their money.

While these studies are a few years old now, and there is no way to get a study that is 100% accurate, the trend is clear: the vast majority of consumers turn to search engines as a primary source of information for decision making.

Here is the kicker: Over 70% of the results that are clicked are organic; meaning the search engine has chosen to place the results there "naturally" as opposed to the link being a paid advertisement.

When you stop to think about it, this makes sense. Ranking organically is basically like getting a nod of approval from the search engine. It's like a trusted source telling you that this is the best result; this is what you are looking for. And this isn't going to change any time soon, as the search engine ads are now being clearly marked as just that: ads.

This amount of mounting evidence is hard to ignore. So it is no wonder that SEO has become an industry worth billions. But with an industry that size comes a lot of misinformation.

There are many camps in the SEO world. They all have their own theories. They all have their own "ethics." There are the pure "white hat" marketers. There are software engineers that run thousands of tests to find correlations to extrapolate how search engine algorithms work. There are the "black hat" SEOs that try to fool the search algorithms to get quick results. There are even hackers.

The funny thing is, multiple different sources with multiple different viewpoints can all be right depending on what you are trying to achieve.

This is a topic that can get extremely technical. But it doesn't have to be. And for the sake of this chapter, it won't be.

Rather, I want to share with you the ***essence*** of what search engine optimization is and how search engines work to decide what will rank at the top. My hope is that this will help you cut through the clutter, distill the noise, and apply this knowledge to whatever route you decide to take.

You will also see why THIS is the perfect book to get an overview of search engine optimization.

And if you do want to get into the more technical, actionable, nitty-gritty of SEO, you can hop on over to the bonus section **(http://www.buzzergy.com/seo/book-bonus/)** where I provide you with tons of actionable advice that I simply can't fit into one chapter.

Let's hop into it…

Google Is King

When speaking about SEO and gaining rankings, the discussion always circles around Google. It is easy to see why. Google owns more than two thirds of the search market in the U.S.A. And in some countries, such as Germany, they own so much of the market that the government is trying to forcefully access their algorithm to "make sure no one is being cheated."

That's right. Google drives so much business that they impact national economies.

Yes, there are other search engines. But if you can rank on Google chances are you can rank on the others as well. And if you can't rank on those search engines but rank on Google, you'll be doing fine for yourself anyway.

The market around the single entity of Google has gotten so large that there are news sources that specialize in what Google does. And it resembles the real news. Every single change, no matter how big or small, is blown out of proportion.

The second Google makes an algorithm change to decide how they will display their search results, it reverberates through the internet and the talk around the water cooler begins. Even nonstories turn into hysteria for the sake of driving readership.

If Matt Cutts (the head of Google's Web Spam team) sneezes, there are sure to be countless articles analyzing what the sneeze meant.

If you follow along with what people are saying, it would seem that what it takes to rank on Google changes every few months. But the truth is SEO hasn't changed much since its beginnings. Sure, it has become a lot more nuanced. But the core of it remains the same. And the good news is that if you know what you are doing, if you pick up on the nuances, you'll actually leave others in the dust.

This is what we are going to talk about: the timeless things that have worked, work now, and will always work when it comes to the world of rankings and then get into why these things will never change. But first, I have to warn you...

DISCLAIMER: SEO Is A Marketing TACTIC

If you read any SEO forum you might get the sense that SEO is the end-all, be-all. But the truth is, it is a tactic that falls within the greater realm of marketing.

You see, ranking in a search engine simply drives visitors to your website. If you've done your job properly, it drives targeted visitors (potential buyers). But if you get everything else wrong - the web design, copy, lead collection and nurturing, and so on - then your rankings and traffic mean very little in the grand scheme of things.

In fact, if you attract the right visitors but send them to a sub-par page, you will actually damage your business rather than helping it.

This is where many SEOs get it wrong, and where many companies go wrong with hiring SEO services. It should be viewed within the greater context of marketing. It is a part of the mix; not the whole.

Having given you a slew of impressive statistics to start this off, I can honestly tell you that any business that is great at marketing but has no search rankings is far better off than a business that has great rankings but is terrible at marketing.

So if this is your first foray into the world of search rankings then you're in a much better position than most because you are reading this in the midst of a book covering many other high-level marketing topics.

There is even more good news. Rather than getting into the technical minutia and tricks to gain rankings, I am going to explain to you how Google works. And once you understand it you will see that, with just a few tweaks, a lot of actions you can take to benefit your marketing will actually improve your rankings as well.

The Two Main Ingredients Of High Search Rankings

Obtaining good rankings in search engines has always come down to two main ingredients: on-page optimization and off-page optimization.

On-page optimization simply means that you create your web pages in a way that communicates to Google what topic your page is all about. You want to pick good, relevant keywords that people are searching for but preferably aren't that competitive. You also want to place these keywords in the right places on the page.

In the early days of search engines, webmasters could literally stuff their pages with keywords and rank for them. But as I mentioned, good marketing has to prevail. A page full of gibberish isn't going to convince anyone to buy anything. So even if you rank a page like this, it's not really going to lead to any sales.

Site owners wised up to this and started putting white text on white backgrounds in order to stuff the page with keywords for search engines, but hide all the gibberish from users. You see, search engines use something called "spiders" or "robots" to crawl the source code of the page. So even if there is white text on a white background and people can't see it, the search engines can.

Since those early days, Google and site owners have gone back and forth in a battle royal. Site owners find loopholes to rank quickly and Google combats this by updating its algorithm.

It has gotten to a point where you can't really get very much of an advantage by optimizing your on-page content. But **you can prevent yourself from ranking by not having your content up to par**.

In fact, Google has 200 factors they take into account when ranking a site; a good portion of which signal the quality of your site. In other words better content is, for lack of a better word, better. Faster site speed is better. And the list goes on. What's better for your customer is actually better for you and your site's rankings.

As I always say, these days you must: WRITE FOR HUMANS, EDIT FOR SEARCH ENGINES.

The process of keyword research and page optimization is a bit technical, and in the bonus section you will find a guide for this.

When you really get down to it, this part of the process makes total sense. In order to rank for a specific search term, the page you are trying to rank should be about that topic. Simple.

The other part of the search formula - the off-page optimization - is where things get a little bit more complex, and that is where the real battle for rankings resides...

The Off-Page Battle Royal

Much like there was a battle of on-page tricks in the early days, there was also a battle of off-page tricks. This battle continues to this day.

One of the very first signals that Google used to decide where a website should rank is backlinks. Backlinks are links pointing to a site from another site (also called inbound links). So, if the Huffington Post links to your website, you have a backlink from the Huffington Post.

Links are really what the internet is built on. In the early days, before Google, the only way to really navigate from one site to another was to follow links. You would, of course, assume that if a site you are reading is linking to another, that the page being linked to is going to be relevant and possibly worth looking at as well.

To this day, links really drive a lot of the internet. Social networks are essentially built around the sharing of content and links.

As a signal, this makes sense. A link is basically a referral. And when you break it down, Google's algorithm creates what is essentially a large network of referrals.

The more backlinks you have from other websites, the more referrals you have. These websites are vouching for you. They are pointing to you as a source worth visiting/reading.

When you do a search, Google has to show you a list of results. But they don't really "know" any of the companies they are showing. So they do their best at guessing what you might want to see by looking at who is being recommended by others (through links).

SEOs figured this out and started manufacturing these signals. And to be fair, in the early days they were very easy to manufacture. People would build mass links from directories, articles, and forum profiles. When Web 2.0 sites (like Tumblr) came out, so did a lot of software to automate building backlinks from the platforms.

It was all about quantity. That is no longer the case.

This battle for supremacy between Google and SEOs with their tricks has brought us into the current environment...

Modern SEO

In today's world, just building a ton of links to your web pages no longer works. In fact, it will have the opposite effect; you'll get penalized. Google has progressively implemented new guidelines. The ranking game has become more nuanced.

These days, rather than quantity, it is all about quality, relevance, and authority. You want links from quality, highly-authoritative sites within your industry. When you begin to obtain these, you start to build up your own authority. You become relevant in Google's eyes when it comes to certain topics. And ranking becomes much easier.

Think of it in terms of the real world. If you are looking for the best possible oral surgeon, are you more likely to listen to the advice of your dentist or the advice of your plumber? The dentist has authority in this space and a referral from him is far more powerful and trustworthy.

As I mentioned before, links are basically referrals. So getting a few links from sites that have authority in your industry is far more powerful than getting a ton of links from unrelated, low-quality sites.

So how do you get these types of links?

There are two answers. You can go the “black hat” route and manufacture these signals. Or, you can go the “white hat” route and **start marketing**.

The “black hat” route is more technical. This approach usually gets results far quicker. But it is also more risky. *Although, plenty of webmasters who have followed Google’s guidelines explicitly have still been penalized.*

Or you can start gaining rankings by taking actions that are generally going to help your business. Start publishing authoritative content. Start getting in front of your ideal clients. Start networking with other industry influencers. Start getting people to talk about you and your business. And now that you know that links are important - get those people to link to you.

These are things you *should* be doing even if you’ve never considered SEO. But with the two simple tweaks - knowing which keywords you want to go after and obtaining authoritative links - you can start benefiting from these actions even more.

Faking Authority

I think that any discussion of SEO would be incomplete without at least touching on the subject of "black hat" tactics. And I firmly hold the belief that even the whitest of white hat SEOs should familiarize themselves with these tactics because (1) they are a major part of the industry and (2) they give a lot of insight into what is currently working for obtaining search results.

You can look at the two opposing approaches in these terms...

White Hat SEO leverages the natural authority you build in order to gain rankings. Black Hat works in the opposite direction, by quickly getting rankings and then hopefully leveraging the new traffic to build authority over time.

Essentially, black hat tactics allow you to **fake authority before you actually achieve it**.

After all, Google's robots just scan the internet and analyze the sites based on a set of signals. They can't do much subjective judging. So they can be fooled.

I have more than dabbled in both forms of SEO and everything in between on the spectrum. And I harness no guilt about "gaming" the system. Google often goes against its own motto of "don't be evil" and pulls the rug from under small businesses that followed the word of Google like gospel.

The point is, you should take the approach that you feel comfortable taking. But just because you don't want to execute "black hat" tactics, it doesn't mean that you shouldn't educate yourself and apply them in a "white hat" manner.

If you want to be as safe as possible, here is a good rule of thumb: a safe link is one that has the potential of sending direct, targeted traffic to your site. This is a link that could help you even when you take rankings out of the equation.

Establish The Foundations And Start Growing

As I previously mentioned, SEO is a method. And it just so happens to fall in line nicely with other methods that you should be taking action on if you are marketing your business online.

Make sure that your website is up to par. Have a way to collect leads, use sales copy where it is appropriate, optimize your website for conversions, and so on. But also include the factors that are necessary to start ranking for keywords that attract your ideal customer.

When you really boil it down, SEO hasn't changed much since its beginnings. It comes down to content and backlinks. This is something that has always been true and will continue to be so for the foreseeable future. But it is the marriage of good SEO and good overall marketing that will grow your business.

If you're ready to start optimizing your website, to build yourself up as an authority, and to get your share of Google's traffic windfall, check out all the actionable bonus content that I have available for you at no cost here: http://www.buzzergy.com/seo/book-bonus/.

About Eugene Farber

Eugene Farber is a marketing consultant specializing in content marketing and search engine optimization. He has helped everyone from solo recruiters to international education organizations drive more business through higher rankings on Google. You can get more actionable ranking and marketing advice, and get a FREE copy of the “Content Optimization Guide” here:

http://www.buzzergy.com/seo/book-bonus/.

CHAPTER 12

The "Hello" Strategy: Why Good Marketing Tactics Mean Never Saying "Goodbye"

Meny Hoffman

The Best Way To Improve Your Modern Marketing Methods? Include Old-Fashioned, Proven Techniques In Your Marketing Plan

As this article is penned, millions of people across the globe are eagerly waiting to get their hands on yet another newly released version of the iPhone. While this paragraph is being typed, visitors are flooding the Toys

"R" Us website to reserve a set of the recently updated Skylanders Trap Team toy series. In the time it takes to complete this article, luxury department store Harrods will have already closed the pre-order list on a limited-edition luxury stroller line created by famed British carmaker Aston Martin.

Are you seeing a pattern here?

The mindset of every human being is wired to consistently desire something new. Something different. Something better. And that's perfectly fine when you're dealing with electronics, toys and prams - do away with the old, usher in the new. However, the same can't be said when it comes to the topic of marketing.

This is a subject I often stumble across when discussing business challenges with fellow entrepreneurs. So many folks are stuck in a mindset that believes new technology can somehow replace traditional marketing efforts that are oh-so-important, and as of late, oh-so-forgotten.

You see, with all the mesmerizing glitz and glamour created by modern marketing platforms like digital advertising and social media, traditionally-successful mediums like direct mail or print advertisements have fallen to the wayside. They've been abandoned. But for many small business owners, the good ol' fashioned way of promoting brand values and generating exposure may actually help amplify the outcome of those newer, more modern marketing initiatives that you've eagerly embraced.

Instead of viewing those dated methods as obsolete, consider adding them to your marketing mix and maximizing the value of both the old and the new.

Sing The Praises Of Print Ads

There are those who'd like to think that print advertisements have gone the way of fax machines, rolodexes and tape cassette players. Between Google AdWords and AdSense banner ads, you can speedily promote your message to the world at the click of a mouse. This is an era when whole magazines are published exclusively online and digital newspapers are read on mobile devices - who still looks at traditional print ads?

You'd be surprised at just how popular they are and how many hi-tech Fortune 500 companies swear by them. Print still has its virtues and, when harnessed as a tool within the marketing ecosystem, can be used as part of a larger effort to draw the public toward interactive, tablet, mobile and social media initiatives. But don't take my word for it - look at what media giant CBS recently pulled off.

To promote the CBS lifestyle and fashion publication, Watch Magazine, the media conglomerate commissioned an international violin virtuoso named Charlie Siem to compose and perform a special musical score - not for a cinematic film or stirring opera, but for the magazine brand itself. Siem's sensational soundtrack was then promoted heavily among the magazine's glossy, color-rich pages.

While the ads touted the historic nature of this endeavor - lauded as the first score ever created for a print publication - the primary objective was to direct readers to the Watch Magazine website, where they could listen to the composition, view behind-the-scenes footage, and learn more about the CBS brand as a whole. Although this campaign was clearly predicated on a print-based platform, the nature of its flexible blueprint quickly transitioned into an all-encompassing, comprehensive user experience designed to imperceptibly educate readers about other CBS initiatives.

Amplifying print ad outcomes is not limited solely to the world of music. The following interactive concept created by the Ultimate Fighting Championship (UFC) took more of a hands-on trajectory.

To endorse an upcoming sporting event taking place between two martial arts champions, the UFC created print ads featuring a 3-foot-long, paper replica of an Ultimate Fighting Championship belt. Magazine viewers could cut out the chiseled gold belt with scissors and wear it like a real champion. And that was just the beginning. The ad encouraged viewers to visit a Facebook page where, after posting a photo of themselves wearing the belt, they'd get a chance to win coveted tickets to the UFC event.

The hundreds of thousands of enthusiastic responses they got from this plain old magazine ad was nothing short of astounding. And eye-opening.

It behooves us to examine the way we use print ads and reevaluate how they are employed. No longer are they a linear, one-dimensional tool that ends up in the trash can after a day or two. The humble print ad as we know it is a critical partner in the complex marketing ecosystem - and when treated as such, can yield impressive results.

But the print ad is hardly alone and shares the stage with yet another much-maligned, completely misunderstood marketing implement: the postcard.

Stack Those Cards In Your Favor

According to a survey conducted by Target Marketing, the channel delivering the strongest Return on Investment (ROI) for customer acquisition was overwhelmingly direct mail. While many of today's digital marketing techniques are often geared toward younger or affluent audiences, direct mail effortlessly transcends demographics and easily reaches people of all ages, income brackets and ethnicities.

Believe it or not, this seemingly overlooked marketing method is actively being used by North America's leading corporations to generate new leads and boost customer retention levels.

Now granted: simply mailing out a giant postcard with your company name and phone number won't do the trick. You've got to apply the same thought and creativity that digital marketing requires - and adapt it for use on a piece of paper bearing a postage stamp. The key is to attach incentive or value to the mailing - be it a postcard, letter or anything else that fits in a mailbox -

and grab the viewer's attention in a previously unexpected way.

The Farmers Insurance Group sent out a postcard that took this concept literally. On the front of each postcard was a mini bumper sticker which could be peeled off and actually placed on a car. While on the topic of automobiles, Toyota turned thousands of heads by mailing out small rectangular postcards to announce the launch of its new Camry sedan. There was just one small catch: the only thing printed on the card was a giant QR code shaped as the silhouette of a car. The code linked to a special landing page where viewers could see photos of the new car, request a free brochure, or even schedule a test drive at a local dealership. It was so intriguing that many recipients who didn't have smartphones reportedly asked friends who did to scan the QR code and see where it led.

An international campaigning and advocacy organization called ONE began planting seeds in people's minds with a special postcard mailing that was sent out containing - you guessed it - plantable carrot seeds embedded inside the paper and a headline blaring: "Sow the seeds of change!" The message was to promote sustainable farming programs; the outcome had competing organizations absolutely green with envy.

Not ready to spend extra money jazzing up your postcards with carrot seeds? That's perfectly fine. The point here is not to encourage backyard gardening as a hobby; it's to emphasize that direct mailings perform amazingly well when you merge them with other marketing tools or create an out-of-the-box idea that reinvents the way these cards are traditionally used.

From Coupon To Groupon To You

The very first coupon was created in 1887 and the concept was met with critical acclaim. In recent times though, many began to view the voucher platform as outdated. Just when everybody began cheering the demise of the trusty paper coupon, a company called Groupon took the digital world by storm and transplanted the old-fashioned coupon concept into the cyberspace arena.

But who says coupons have to provide discounts only? Steve Gadlin, an enterprising artist who draws nothing but silly-looking, stick-figure cats, used Groupon to promote his own skills. "I want to draw a cat for you. If you think $3 is cheap, you're right. It's a 70% discount... these felines are usually $10!" wrote Steve is his humorous coupon. Over 920 people bought Groupon's self-described "confusing holiday gift" and Steve, banking on the resulting publicity, ultimately appeared on Shark

Tank and bagged a $25,000 investment from celebrity Mark Cuban.

Then you've got the fishing gear retailer in California who mailed out T-Shirts to a select group of clientele with a coupon offering them a free fishing rod with any purchase. The only catch? The coupon was printed on the garment. You'd have to arrive wearing the T-Shirt so a cashier could scan the giant UPC code stamped across your chest.

Of course, if you're a purist who prefers to go with paper coupons, know that you're in good company. Office Depot mailed out a very interesting type of paper coupon - a three-foot tall, brown paper bag that, when unfolded, displayed this bold message: "Get 15% off everything you can fit in this bag!" Below the headline sat a UPC code for the cashier to scan at checkout and issue the 15% discount. This hybrid coupon was evidently hard to ignore... and even harder to lose.

Again, the lesson here is obvious: take a traditional marketing medium, beef it up with some modern creativity, and you'll go places.

The Lowdown On Going Hi-Tech

We all know that data is king. The more you know about customers, the better chance you'll have at profiting from them.

There are various software programs available that can provide you with unprecedented opportunities to better understand your customers. Take one glance at the dashboard and you'll be inundated with real-time website analytics, statistical click-through techniques, retention modeling methods and sophisticated growth algorithms. These programs were crafted by leading computer engineers and marketing executives to help the growing business accurately gauge what customers want and need.

But there's a potential danger here.

When we become so intent on using hi-tech computations or mathematical algorithms to mine data about the people using our product or service, we often neglect to remember the most important thing of all: that they are human begins.

People want to feel connected with and spoken to and valued as having a personal relationship with your brand. Not poked, prodded and examined under a microscope like a biological specimen in a laboratory. So yes, while it is important that you invest in a reputable CRM system and manage your metrics, it's just as critical to invest time communicating one-on-one with your customers to learn what they like - and more considerably, what they don't - about your brand. And ultimately, telling your customers that you've heard their voice and will really be acting on their input.

The famous Domino's Pizza campaign is a good example that instantly comes to mind.

After using the same tried-and-true recipe for over forty years, the franchise began to get wind of complaints. Tastes were changing, expectations had become higher due to the influx of newer pizzeria chains pushing bolder flavors and diverse toppings, and people were seeking a superior pizza experience.

Instead of dismissing the criticism as hollow comments spoken by only a minority of patrons, the company actually paid for customers to visit its headquarters in Michigan and tell executives in person how they felt about Domino's Pizza. There were hundreds of complaints regarding the flavor and texture - and about the crust in particular. The company asked for feedback, listened to it carefully, and spent millions to create a new pizza recipe for its nearly 9,000 franchises across the globe. Domino’s then launched a series of advertisements featuring long time customers and employees acknowledging the antiquated recipe was downright stale. The ads announced that a dynamic new recipe was created based on the dialogue started with Domino's customers, and showed the company was working hard to accommodate the tastes desired by their clientele.

The 14.3% increase in revenue during the first quarter after launching this campaign - and resulting 400% rise in company stock since the new recipe was implemented - dramatically illustrates that the best, most genuine feedback comes directly from the people you serve.

Here's another intriguing point to consider.

Just about every respectable business these days has, at the very least, a Facebook page or Twitter feed. One of the first things I'll hear when this topic arises is: "So how can I get more likes on Facebook?" The next refrain is equally irritating: "What can I write on Twitter to make folks repost it?" It's disturbing to see that so many businesspeople view social media as nothing more than a uni-directional medium to blatantly promote themselves and trumpet messages loudly to the entire world.

Instead of shouting, how about listening?

According to the Aberdeen Group Report published in Forbes, while 86% of companies use social media as a marketing tool, only 41% use it for communicating directly with customers. While marketing pushes information out, to truly understand customers, companies have to start by taking information in.

Maker's Mark, a small-batch bourbon whiskey distiller based in Kentucky, accomplished that beautifully. The company was experiencing a crisis of sorts. Demand was extremely high and Maker's Mark couldn't produce their secret brew fast enough. The solution? Reduce the already-high, 90 proof alcohol content to a still-high 84 proof level, so they could mass-produce the spirit faster and ship it to loyal customers without delay. No sooner had the company formally issued an announcement of their intention, the Maker's Mark twitter feed exploded in protest, with angry tweets from the public objecting to the planned move.

The marketing team at Maker's Mark immediately took note of the maddening chatter and reached out to commentators to understand why people were so vehemently opposed to the change. After that initial outreach, despite the supply constraints and distribution issues, Maker's Mark decided to acquiesce to the demands of devoted customers by not reducing the alcohol content. The team went forward, knowing full well their decision would affect sales projections and possibly diminish short-term profits. But they knew, even more importantly, that keeping their customer-base happy was paramount.

This wise decision was not made by scrutinizing countless sheets of consumer data algorithms or examining color-coded bar charts. It was accomplished by communicating directly with customers in a genuine, personal, human manner.

From Basic Learning To Actual Doing

You've just read a number of real-life examples illustrating how companies of various sizes tapped into the power of traditional marketing philosophies and modern business techniques. They chose to embrace the old and the new concurrently.

Take note: You too, can enjoy the best of both worlds.

You can collectively adopt the mindset of viewing each component, be it old-fashioned or new-fangled, as a specific tool within the marketing ecosystem. Spend time creating strategies for integrating the time-tested methods of the past with the promising business practices of the future. Go forward and warmly welcome every technique, no matter how aged or how young, into your ever-expanding marketing arsenal .

The word "goodbye" doesn't belong in the business lexicon.

About Meny Hoffman

Meny Hoffman is the CEO of Ptex Group, an award-winning marketing and business services agency headquartered in Brooklyn, NY. A longtime entrepreneur, he specializes in creating strategic marketing solutions and business-boosting tactics to help growing businesses achieve higher levels of success. Meny can be reached at **mhoffman@ptexgroup.com** or follow **@menyhoffman** on twitter.

To join Meny's Let Talk Business™ newsletter and have insightful articles like this sent to your inbox on a regular basis, visit **http://www.ptexgroup.com/lets-talk**

CHAPTER 13

"How To Turn Your Relationships Into More Revenues And Clients"

John Corcoran

"You are the average of the five people you spend the most time with." - Jim Rohn

Can I be honest here? I love and I hate that quote. I love it because it is true. But I also hate it because it's so unspecific.

People hear that quote and they think "Oh, wow. That's really true!" Then they go back to doing what they

were doing because they don't know how to implement the principle behind the quote in the real world.
In this chapter, I want to provide a 7-step system I have developed for implementing this famous Jim Rohn quote. I will explain how to go about identifying, locating, reach out to, and ultimately building relationships with those five people. I will explain a system for first identifying the people who you want to build relationships with, then reaching out to them, and finally building a relationship with them over time.

Let's be clear about one thing though: building relationships is not a quick process. If you are looking for an overnight solution, you won't find one here. But... if you put in the time, then your network will pay huge dividends. And your network will never go out style, become obsolete, or need an upgrade.

Why Relationships Matter

Jeff Rose is not your typical financial planner. In fact, as an Army Staff Sergeant for the Illinois Army National Guard, he led a division of nine other men into battle in the early years of the War in Iraq.

That's right folks: he can explain the details of annuities to you, and he can operate an M-4 rifle. Better pay attention, right?

The experience taught him many lessons: the importance of working hand-in-hand with teammates, building relationships with your team, and helping one another. “Early on during training, it was embarrassing. We couldn’t function as a team,” says Rose. Over time, Rose and the other members of his platoon got to know each other better and their relationships gelled. “Everything started to click and then by the end of our tour in Iraq, we were a machine.”

It was a lesson that Rose applied years later when he had returned to the private sector. When Rose started his own financial planning firm, he knew he needed a way to stand out so that he could attract clients. That’s when he started a blog.

“I had just left my big firm so I was just looking for unique ways to market myself,” says Rose. “I read a financial planning trade magazine, and they had an article about if you want to stand out from the crowd of other financial advisors, then you need to start a blog. I didn’t even know what a blog was, but I was determined to figure it out.”

But Rose soon found blogging wasn’t as easy as it seemed. “There was some growth early on, but not much,” says Rose. “If I got 100 people to my blog, I was blown away.”

He quickly learned if he wanted to actually land clients with his blog, he would need to do more than simply writing regularly.

That's when Rose started building relationships with other financial planners who were bloggers. Rose found a mentor -- another financial advisor at his former firm. "He gave me guidance. He showed me how it was done."

Shortly after that, Rose joined a private forum with other bloggers who provided critical advice and support. This little community of other personal finance bloggers became a crucial source of support, guidance, and friendship.

Jeff Rose's story is a common one, because his experience demonstrates the importance of teamwork if you want to attract clients and grow your revenues as a business owner. Like an army platoon going in to battle, you need a team. You cannot go it alone.

How To Systemize Your Relationship Building

As I mentioned, I have developed a 7-step process I'll share with you for building relationships and growing your network.

First, I will go over the seven steps. Then I'll dive into how you can apply them to growing your business.

Here are the seven steps:

1. Develop a Mindset of Helping Others First
2. Create a Roadmap to Your Future
3. Before Reaching Out, Lay the Foundation Using Social Media
4. How to Email Busy VIPs and Get a Response Every Time
5. Get Offline and Start Attending Conferences and Events
6. Create a System for Following Up
7. How to Measure ROI and Optimize Your System

OK, now, let's take a look at how to apply these steps.

1. Develop A Mindset Of Helping Others First

One of the biggest barriers for anyone who is trying to build a business is not that they don't know any one of significance who might be valuable to their business, or that they don't have anything to "offer" the VIPs or Influencers who they meet. The problem is they are thinking too much of themselves, rather than of others.

That can sound confusing. How can you build your *own* business if you're supposed to focus on helping others?

It's simple. Help others, and they will help you. Or, as Zig Ziglar said, "You can have everything in life you want, if you will just help other people get what they want."

Jeff Rose says it took him awhile after starting his own business to realize the importance of helping others first. "I think at the beginning I didn't quite get it. I was being somewhat selfish," says Rose. As an example, Rose approached the Art of Manliness blog and pitched himself to be profiled in their "So You Want My Job" series, because the site had not previously featured a financial planner.

"I emailed and said I love the blog and you've never done a 'So You Want My Job' profile on a financial advisor - and I offered myself," says Rose, who laughs at the memory. In spite of his approach, Rose landed the profile. "It was very self-serving at the time. If I did it again, I'd do it differently today."

2. Create A Roadmap To Your Future

You wouldn't leave the house for a 1,000-mile journey without a map, would you? Of course not. You wouldn't make it very far.

In business, your relationships make up the roads and highways that guide your journey. You can't get to your end destination without them.

And yet most people embark on the journey of their career, or try to build a business, without taking time to map out their route. They spend almost no time thinking about how they should build relationships to support their journey -- even though those relationships are one of the most critical factors in a person's success or failure.

They leave relationships up to - dare I say it? - chance. *Gasp!*

And then they wonder why their career or business hasn't taken off.

So do the opposite: create your own roadmap. Your relationships roadmap. **Sit down and create a list of the 50+ people who you want to build a deeper relationship with over the course of the next 12 months.**

I call this your 'Conversations List' because you should think of it as a list of people who you want to have an ongoing conversation with over time. You can do this by creating a very simple spreadsheet using Google Drive or Microsoft Excel.

You don't need to include much information, so it shouldn't take you more than 20 minutes to create an initial list. Just include some basic details, like name and company. I also like to write down how I can be of help to that particular person.

Who should be on your list? Include both people who you know already and who you want to deepen your relationship with, and people who you don't know at all. Include professionals in your local community and perhaps a few thought leaders in your area of expertise.

But don't just include people who are already successful. "Often people think that networking is all about connecting with people who are bigger or more successful than they are," says Corbett Barr, CEO and co-founder of Fizzle.co, an online business training program. "But actually you should focus often on people who are at about your level. Some of my most meaningful relationships have been with people who are at your same level."

Barr also says you should try to connect with others who are go-getters with a good work ethic. "Spot people in your peer group that are standouts and become friends with them," he says.

I suggest a variety approach - include a lot of other professionals who are "at your level," but also include some people you admire who are further on the journey and who you think you can help out.

You can create a similar list for organizations you are interested in participating in and events you want to attend. I'd suggest a much smaller "Conversations list" of 6-8 organizations and 6-8 events you'd like to involve yourself with over time.

3. Before Reaching Out, Lay the Foundation Using Social Media

Before you dash off an email to some VIP you are hoping to become your new BFF, hold your horses a minute. Slow things down. You don't ask to get married before asking for a first date.

So take some time to lay a little foundation.

Let's pretend you're back in high school, and you want to meet a new girl or guy. Do you walk right up to him or her and introduce yourself? Probably not, right?

Instead, you try to work your way in. You find ways to have a few short conversations in the halls or the cafeteria. Then, once he or she has seen your face around awhile, you are no longer some anonymous person they don't know.

Social media works the same way. You can use it to show your face around and exchange short messages so that when you go in for that direct email, you're not some anonymous stranger.

The key here is to use the platform where the person is most active, not *your* social media platform of choice. You may prefer Facebook, but if the person you want to connect with is most active on Instagram, then that's where you need to be.

For example, let's say you are a local social media consultant advising local businesses in your community on how to use social media to get more customers and sales. if you wanted to connect with Facebook marketing wizard Amy Porterfield, you're more likely to make a *personal* connection with her on her Instagram account, because she's actually more active there than on Facebook.

Whatever the platform, look out for opportunities to help, or reply to a request for feedback.

4. How To Email Busy VIPs And Get A Response

Assuming you have already laid the foundation and "warmed up" the relationship using social media, then you've already done the heavy lifting. Now you need to contact the person. There are four key principles to connecting with people who may be as busy or busier than you are.

The four principles are:

- **Do Your Research**
- **Keep it Short**
- **Focus on THEM**
- **Have a Clear Call to Action**

One of the best books I've read on how to email busy people was originally published in 1936. It's called *How to Win Friends and Influence People* by Dale Carnegie.

Of course, Carnegie didn't know he was writing a book that would apply to email, which would not be invented for another 40+ years. But the principles in the book are universally applicable, whether you are connecting with someone in-person, over the phone, or via email.

"Of course, you are interested in what you want. You are eternally interested in it," wrote Carnegie. "But no one else is. The rest of us are just like you: we are interested in what we want."

Corbett Barr says that when you email someone, you should entice their self-interest by grabbing their attention. "Lead with your best foot forward, whether by name dropping or key facts, such ""my podcast gets 50,000 downloads a month, and I'd love to have you on as a guest,'" says Barr.

Another approach is to try to land a big name first, then to use that to reel in others. For example, if you were creating an interview series, you might say something like "I'd love to get 15 minutes of your time to participate in the interview series, and I'm going to make it really easy for you," says Barr. "Oh, and by the way, ZenHabits - " a website TIME Magazine recognized as one of the top 50 websites of 2011 - " founder Leo Baubauta has confirmed he's participating as well."

One last tip: "Pull out and make bold the thing you're asking them to do," says Barr. "Often you have to read five paragraphs to figure out what the ask is."

5. Get Offline And Start Attending Conferences And Events

Another thing you should absolutely do is to get out of your office and crawl out from behind your laptop and start meeting people.

If you live in a small town, this is even more important. Start traveling to conferences and conventions.

You'll make great friends and meet partners who you can work with as your business grows.
Whatever you do, don't expect to build as solid relationships with people without meeting them in person. I believe you get to know someone far better once you meet face-to-face.

6. Create A System For Following Up

The next step is to create a system for following up. One of the biggest mistakes I see people make after meeting someone is failing to follow up.

Here's how it happens: you meet someone at a conference or other event. You have a good conversation and maybe you think "this is someone cool."

And then... nothing.

You don't follow up with that person. And they don't follow up with you. It's as if you never met.

Do you realize how crazy a strategy this is, especially if you don't like networking? By not following up, it's like you're dooming yourself to the "networking hamster wheel."

If you want to go pro, you need a system for following up and managing relationships. If you have a system for following up, it helps ensure you spend time following up and deepening your relationship with the people who matter.

Now, you can try to schedule reminders in your calendar manually, but that will get unwieldy quickly. A much better approach is to use a CRM program (which stands for “customer relationships management”) to manage your relationships and automate reminders to followup.

There are literally dozens of CRMs, and more and more of them have been aiming at the small solopreneur market. These include Insightly, Podio, Nimble, and larger options traditionally used by sales people like Salesforce.com.

I use a tool called Contactually.com which I love because it’s helps me manage thousands of relationships in minimal time. They have a free 30-day trial you can try out.

Here's how it works: you sync your email account, your LinkedIn, Facebook, and other social media profiles, and then Contactually creates merged profiles for all of your contacts. You then prioritize people into what they call "buckets," based off how frequently you want to follow up with that person. Contactually will send you reminders to follow up at that interval.

7. How To Measure ROI And Optimize Your System

Finally, you need to be able to figure out if all of this is worthwhile, or a waste of time. In other words, whether you're actually turning those people you're connecting with into more income for your business.

To figure that out, practice keeping track of any incoming business or professional referrals for 30 days. This is going to be easiest if you sell a service like coaching or web design, but it can also work if you sell digital products as well.

Create a simple Google Drive document that includes the first and last name or the business name of the new client or buyer and the referral source. The referral source could be a person, or an organization or a conference where that new client came from.

Now here's the key point. Over time, you will be able to see patterns emerge. You will be able to see what referral source is actually accounting for a large portion of your revenue.

Pay attention to these patterns. Not only will you see which relationships are bearing the most fruit, but you'll also see which relationships are most useful or which conferences, or meetups you attended yielded the best payback.

You can also figure out which organizations you should remain involved with - or better yet, deepen your involvement with. Then you can double down, or cut out what doesn't yield results.

Now Go Out and Build Your Network

There are no secrets to getting a flood of powerful connections and friends overnight.

If you want to break through, then you need to focus on building relationships. But if you are willing to put in the time and effort, your relationships will be an asset that fuels your business for years to come.

About John Corcoran

John Corcoran is a former Clinton White House Writer and founder of **SmartBusinessRevolution.com,** where he writes about how to increase your income by building and nurturing relationships with people who matter. You can download his free, 52-page ebook, How to Increase Your Income Today by Building Relationships with Influencers, Even if You Hate Networking, at **http://smartbusinessrevolution.com/free-ebook.**

CHAPTER 14

How To Have More Frequent, More Effective Sales Conversations

Matthew Kimberley, Head of the Book Yourself Solid School of Coach Training and Founder of the School for Selling

To be able to sell is one of the most valuable skills you will ever acquire.

When you can sell, you will never be homeless. You will never be unemployed. You will never want for anything.

When you can sell - and when you're selling the right thing to the right people - you will forge your own path in life and answer to nobody.

So study this short chapter with great intent. Take its valuable and easy-to-implement lessons and apply them to your own life, starting right now.

In time, you'll come to enjoy the great game of selling. You get paid when you win. And when you don't win, you don't lose.

It's quite beautiful.

***

Very early on in my career, when I first got started helping out small business owners, one of my promises was that anybody working with me would get more clients.

Everybody wants more clients, right?

But I was having problems: I couldn't deliver on that promise and I didn't know what to do about it. I was stuck.

I was even more stuck because I couldn't work out what I was doing wrong. In fact, I was convinced I was doing everything right. The results told a different story.

I'd had no problem in my previous career, running a busy recruitment agency. I just couldn't replicate the results with my own clients' businesses.

I'd get on the phone with them and we'd sketch out what their business looked like today, and what they wanted it to look like tomorrow.

Then we'd do some strategizing. We'd work out if what they were selling was a good fit for their market. We'd work out if their pricing was a good fit for their business and for their customers. We'd examine the various marketing options they had ...

Then, I'd write a business prescription and they would, most of the time, go off and put those changes in place.

We'd touch base again after a few weeks and look at those numbers again.

And when those numbers were the same, or - heaven forbid - even worse than before, I'd scratch my head and examine my recommendations for flaws, I'd look for holes in my strategy and problems with my solutions.

"I've done everything that you recommended, Matthew," they'd say, "but I still haven't been able to bring any more clients on board."

This was, of course, terrible news. It was terrible news for my clients, terrible news for me, and awful news for my reputation.

Then, one day, frustrated with one of my clients' lack of results (and unfairly taking it out on him) I blurted out "and exactly how many sales conversations have you had since we last spoke?"

His answer was hesitant: "umm, none at all."

I fell off my chair.

"So we're doing all of this business design, all of this branding work, all of this marketing activity, and you're not capitalizing on any of it?" I sputtered.

"But I kind of hoped, Matthew," he replied, "that with all of this in place I wouldn't need to have any sales conversations. I was hoping that the orders would come in thick and fast and that I wouldn't have to do anything more."

At which point I got off the floor, dusted myself down and realized I needed to make some immediate changes to the way I worked.

"Next time we meet," I said, "I'm going to ask you exactly the same question. I'm going to ask you 'How many sales conversations have you had since we last spoke?' and for your sake I hope the number is greater than zero."

When we spoke again, of course, revenue had increased and the number of sales conversations he was having each week were the reason for the increase.

This basic measurement of sales activity is something that small business owners and the self-employed are very bad at doing. Every salaried salesperson at every company in the world has a boss keeping an eye on his key numbers: how many leads, how many offers, how many sales?

But when we're our own bosses, we let ourselves off the hook. We wing it and hope for the best. We figure that the restrictions and structures of the bigger companies don't apply to us.

We are wrong.

The most effective way to dramatically increase your sales results is to keep track of your sales activity. If you know that once a week you've got to report the

number of sales conversations you've had, or the number of offers you've made, to your boss, you're going to make certain that you're not turning up empty-handed to those review meetings.
So that's step number one: start keeping track of everything. Report to somebody - perhaps your coach, perhaps your mastermind group, perhaps your husband or wife, on a weekly basis. Just measuring it will have a discernible strengthening effect on your sales muscle.

Your sales muscle is like all other muscles: it needs to be exercised if it's going to grow.

That means you need good form. Doing any kind of exercise with bad form is a terrible idea. You'll end up doing more harm than good and likely cause some irreparable damage.

You learn good form with study and practice. Read books, join a program like my School for Selling, listen to audio programs. There are hundreds and thousands of books out there that are written exclusively for you, the salesperson. Read some. Apply what you learn. Improve you form.

But form on its own is insufficient. You need frequency as well. How many reps are you doing? Now that you're measuring them, you'll know how many you need to do to get the result you want. Often, the simple answer is "more".

So ... measure your sales activity, get better at it and do more of it.

So far so simple, right?

Yes. Precisely.

There's this dangerous notion out there that selling is difficult, or selling is complicated, or selling is for experts only. That's not true and if you subscribe to that idea you'll never achieve the results you're looking for.

Sales is incredibly easy.

If it wasn't easy you wouldn't see girl scouts selling cookies. If they can do it, so you can you.

Here's how:

First, you identify the people who want what you're selling. If nobody wants what you're selling, then you've got a problem.

You've got an even bigger problem, though, if you've convinced yourself that nobody wants what you're selling without any data to back it up.

I spoke to a lady - a life-coach - who came to one of my workshops. She told me that she was on the verge of giving up on her dream because people weren't interested in paying her for her services.

I asked her which people she was talking about, specifically, and she said "well, everybody. Every time I make an offer they tell me that they don't want to spend any money".

There were a number of reasons, of course, that this could have been happening. Perhaps she was talking to the wrong people? Perhaps she was making offers too early, before people had a chance to get to know her? Perhaps her pricing was whacky? Perhaps her sales conversations were aggressive and pushy? Perhaps she had bad breath?

But it was something else. It was self-delusion.

"So how many times - specifically - has this happened?" I asked.

Her answer? Six times. She had based her entire existential crisis on the fact that she hadn't made a sale to the first six people - the only six people - she had spoken to.

So don't decide whether or not there's a group of people who want to buy what you're selling, instead go out and find out for sure.

When you've identified the people who will buy what you're selling, you then need to do a sufficient amount of marketing to get their interest.

But remember: marketing doesn't get you clients.

That's one of the most important practical considerations of the Book Yourself Solid® small-business client-getting system that I teach.

(Book Yourself Solid® is a book that was created by my business partner: New York Times bestselling author Michael Port, who has helped hundreds of thousands of small business owners like you get more clients than they can handle. You should buy a copy of the book.)

Marketing doesn't get you clients. All that marketing does is create awareness about who you are and what you have to offer the world. It drives eyeballs to your website or footsteps to you door.

It's what you do *after you've got them to your door* that gets you clients.

How many sales conversations you with these people depends on how good you are at turning a lead (a new person potentially interested in what you've got) into a prospect (person definitely interested in what you're selling).

But if you haven't got any leads to convert into prospects, then you can't even get started.

So make sure that the sole purpose of your marketing is to collect contact details from potentially interested parties.

That means you might like to reconsider sponsoring that golf tournament. That means you should reassess whether jumping on the next social-media bandwagon and building an enormous army of passive followers is going to help or hinder your lead-generation efforts. That means you might like to re-prioritize redesigning your website as less important than picking up the phone and talking to some people.

Once you know that you can "switch on" lead flow with a marketing system, it's time to start lining up the sales conversations.

The ideal sales conversation is exactly that: a conversation with somebody who has put up their hand said "I'm potentially interested in buying something, let's talk."

You will derive considerably more satisfaction and enjoy considerably more success if both parties are on the same page.

Here's how to do it properly:

1. Warm your prospect up with enough information and reason to know you, like you and trust you. We only ever make investments when trust exists.

You can do this by email, or by letter, or in-person. I strongly recommend that you don't give any "one-to-one" attention to your prospects at this point, though. Wait for somebody to raise their hand and say "I'm interested in spending some money" before you invest your time in a one-to-one meeting or conversation.

2. Let your prospects know that you have investible opportunities for them.

"I have a variety of paid packages that might solve your problem. Contact me if you're interested in becoming a customer" is an excellent way of doing this. You've made it clear you'll be talking about money upfront and nobody will be under any other kind of illusions.

3. Have sales conversation.

And there's the last part: the crucial part, the part that we all get stuck on so frequently.

(Incidentally, I've had more than one person say to me in the past that they are afraid of offending their prospect by asking them to buy. I have never heard anything so ridiculous in my entire life. When was the last time you got offended when somebody asked you to buy something?).

Start each sales conversation by reminding them - and you - that the purpose of the conversation is to see if they want to buy something.

"So we're talking today because you wanted more information about the Acme drainage service, right? Great! I'll ask you a few questions. If I think I can help you I'll tell you how. Then at the end of this call you decide - yes or no - if you want to go ahead and become a customer today. Does that sound ok to you?"

You've set the stage perfectly and you've told them to expect to make a decision.

They've agreed to that, so you can move on and make your offer:

"On the basis of what you've told me today I believe I can help you. Would you like that? Shall we get started?"

Congratulations. You've just made a highly effective sales call, whether you got a "yes" or a "no".

Now do more of them. In time, you'll get more people saying "yes", but only if you measure your results, work on your form, work on your frequency ... and don't forget to have fun.

It's all a game and you deserve to enjoy it.

About Matthew Kimberley

To have more fun in business and learn more from Matthew, get his free guide:

5 Things You Need To Do Every Morning To Get More Clients In 60 Days

http://www.matthewkimberley.com/how-to-get-more-clients/

CHAPTER 15

How To Get New Clients By Leveraging The World's Largest Social Network

Joseph Bushnell

Your ideal customer is using Facebook right now.

How can I make such a bold assumption? I don't even know what you do or who your ideal target customer is.

Well consider this, at the time of writing this...

- There are more than 1.3 billion monthly users on Facebook (Making it the biggest social network of them all)

- 829 million people log on to Facebook on any given day
- The average Facebook user spends up to 40 minutes per day using the site
- There are 1 billion mobile users on Facebook

The sheer volume of people using the site means that every demographic is covered. I don't care if your typical customers are male, female, young, old, rich, poor, single, married, divorced, gay, straight, college educated, c-level, employee, right wing, left wing, religious, atheist or anything in-between, they are using Facebook.

The people using Facebook span every industry. They have a wide range of hobbies and their interests cover every little area imaginable. No market is untouched.
It's a safe bet that your target audience are using Facebook.

They are spending insane amounts of time on there too. Of course not everyone uses Facebook for 40 minutes per day, that's just an average but again there's a really good chance your target audience use it a lot. Even if they just use it for 5 minutes per day, that's a lot when compared to the average time spent on most other websites or other marketing mediums.

I mean, how often do you spend reading the yellow pages each day?

I rest my case.

Lastly, they use it *everywhere*. 1 billion people are using Facebook not just at home on their laptop or desktop computer but on the move. Their mobile is in their pocket and they are checking Facebook at work, during their lunch break, on the bus, in the doctor's waiting room, at the restaurant and even in bed before they sleep at night.

So that's my case for you marketing on Facebook... Your target audience are using it. They use it often. They use it everywhere they go.

Wouldn't it be cool if you could use this powerful platform to spread the word about your business and attract new customers?

Well, you can!

Yeah, I know, it's not really a big surprise and you probably already knew that. But are you taking advantage of it?

If not, I'd like to challenge you to give it a try because you might just find it becomes an indispensable part of your online lead generation strategy.

Facebook Ads

Rather than messing around, wasting a ton of time trying to get "free traffic", there's a much quicker simpler way to get instant, laser targeted visibility on Facebook and that's by using their advertising platform.

Facebook ads allow you to pay Facebook to reach the news feeds of your target audience instantaneously.

Using Facebook ads you can target your advert so it only gets seen by the people who are most likely to respond to it.

We can do this because Facebook has an incredible amount of data on every user who uses the site. If you have a Facebook account, they already know all about you (yes you!)

They know your name, your age, where you were born, where you live, where you went to school, where you work, what your hobbies are and much more.

How do they know all this?

You told them!

You told them when you filled out your profile information. You told them when you liked certain fan pages or joined certain groups. You told them in the status updates you make.

Also someone else told them. Facebook buys data from 3rd parties too to get to know even more about us.

Now when the average person first hears this it scares them (Oh no, big brother is watching me)

However for us marketers this is a dream come true.

It means we can target our ads so they only get seen by the most relevant people. Very few advertising mediums can offer this.

And personally even as consumer I love Facebook ads. Okay so Facebook has a lot of info on me but they serve me relevant ads, things that matter to me. I don't know about you but I sure prefer relevant ads than irrelevant ones.

The great thing is the advertising platform is *low barrier to entry*. Anyone can use it. You can go set up an account *right now*.

There's pretty much *no minimum spend* either. Whether your budget is big or small, you can advertise on Facebook. If all you have available to spend is a few dollars a day then so be it. If you have a big budget to play with then that's fantastic too, there's certainly no shortage of leads to siphon from Facebook. You can change your budgets at anytime and pause your advertising whenever you like, you're in total control.

Last of all you pay for *results*. Unlike some advertising mediums where you pay regardless of whether you get a response or not, such as radio ads or an ad placed in your local newspaper. With Facebook ads you only pay for results. Most commonly you pay when someone clicks on your ad; you "pay per click".

Or you can choose to pay for impressions (the number of times your ad gets shown) but even that way you are still guaranteed that your ad will be seen a certain amount of times. Its results based and as advertisers seeking a return, it's a pretty good deal for us.

Search vs. Social

Many people who run PPC ads on Google hear about Facebook PPC for the first time and think they are the same thing. Whilst the concept of "paying per click" is the same, they are fundamentally different types of advertising.
I'm a big fan of both these forms of advertising and I wouldn't say one is "better than the other" they're just different and understanding the difference is important.

The main difference between advertising on Google compared with Facebook is the mindset of the person viewing your ad.

When someone is typing in a search query on Google, chances are they are actively looking for something to buy or are at the very least looking to find out more information about a product or service like yours.

However when someone is using Facebook, they are there just socializing or simply browsing because they are bored. They are not there because they are looking to buy something.

So Facebook ads are not as good as Google ads then?

No, that's not what I'm saying. Facebook ads are still incredibly effective; they just need to be approached from a different angle.

Google is based upon real time searches, what that person is looking for in the moment.
Facebook advertising is about who that user *is* as a person.
Facebook ads should be based on what you know about your ideal target audience and then pairing it up with the information Facebook has about its users so you can get your message in front of the most relevant people.

If you get your targeting wrong your ad will seem like an interruption and an annoyance. If you get it right, your ad will seem like "perfect timing". It's all about entering the conversation *already* going on in the mind of your prospect.

I'm a marketing geek. I enjoy it. I think about marketing a lot. I may not do a Google search for the latest marketing software but if I happen to see an ad for it as I'm scrolling my Facebook news feed there's a really good chance I'll be intrigued and will want to know more.

A single male aged 18-30 who is a fan of several sports pages, lads mags and beer might be interested in seeing my gambling advert which has an offer of a free bet.
A couple who have recently just changed their relationship status to "engaged" and live within 10 miles of me, may want to see my wedding photography offer.

A teenage girl who is a fan of practically every single "One Direction" fan page in existence and then see's my one direction t-shirt being advertised may well be interested. She doesn't have to Google it; I just have to know enough about her to know it may be of interest.

It's about the information Facebook can give us about that person and what is going on in their life right now.

The 4 Step Formula For A Winning Facebook Ad

Give yourself the best possible chance for a successful Facebook advertising campaign by following this simple 4 step formula...

1. Establish your goal
2. Create a compelling ad
3. Fine-tune your targeting
4. Improve your ad based on feedback

Establish Your Goal

The first step is to decide upon your goal. What is the end result you are seeking from this advert? If this advert is to be successful you must first *define* success.

Here are some common goals for a Facebook advertising campaign...

- **To gain "Likes"** - You might want to increase the amount of targeted fans on your fan page so that you can get more engagement, activity and social proof.

- **Engagement on a post** - You may have a particular post on your fan page that is more important than the others. You can choose to get more visibility for this post so that it receives more likes, comments, shares and more attention from your audience.

- **Video views** - If you have a video that you want to be seen, there is an option for a "video ad"

- **Event registrants** - You can invite people to a business event that is taking place such as a webinar or live stream in the online world or maybe a seminar or networking event in the real world.

- **To get installs for an app** - If you have a Facebook app or a mobile app in the Apple app store or Google Play store then you can make an ad to encourage people to install your app.

- **Get clicks to a website** - Perhaps you want people to read your latest blog post or go to some other page on your website.

- **To gather leads** - You might want to build your email list so that you can communicate with prospects via email marketing. You can do this by sending people to an opt-in page where you give away something of value in return for their contact details, usually their name and email address but other contact details can be gathered too. Once you have contact details you can create a relationship through email marketing before selling something later on.

- **To make sales** - Perhaps you want to sell something directly. You can either send people to a sales page or you could use a Facebook "offer" where you can give a special discounted price for a limited period of time.

Of course the ultimate goal of any of these objectives is to make a profit. It might be directly or indirectly, in the short term or long term but ultimately that's the aim.

To know whether your campaign was successful or not, you will need to track.

For example...How many likes did you get? How many people signed up for your webinar? How many people joined your email list? How many sales did you make? How many people installed your app?

The reports in your Facebook ads account can give numbers on most of these stats except for goals that are not happening on Facebook itself but over on your own website instead (such as gaining a new email subscriber or making a sale).

If you want to track how many of your email subscribers or sales came as a direct result of your Facebook ads campaign then you will need to use a tracking pixel which is provided by Facebook. You place the pixel on the thank you page of your email subscription or sales page and then you will be able to tell if any new subscribers or customers who reach those pages were because they clicked on your Facebook ad.

Create A Compelling Ad

After you know your goal, you're ready to create your ad. There are many different "types" of ads you can create and they all have their own unique features and nuances but 95% of them boil down to these 4 major components that are common amongst them all...

1. Image
2. Headline
3. Copy
4. Call to action

Image

The very first thing any ad needs to accomplish is to attract attention. After all your ad can't do its job unless it gets noticed in the first place, right?

The easiest way to grab attention with a Facebook ad is to use an eye-catching image. The majority of Facebook ads you create will require an image of some kind unless you are making a video ad.

Use bright colors which will stand out or maybe use an usual picture where someone can't help but do a double take.

Headline

Now that they've noticed your image and you have gained their attention for just a split second you need to keep their attention and peak their interest with your headline. You don't get much room to play with here (a paltry 25 characters at the time of writing this) so there's no room for being creative or clever, dive straight in with your main benefit.

Copy

Next you have a small text area to say what you *really* want to say. This is where you can write a tiny amount of "micro copy" up to 90 characters long to entice the reader into being interested enough to want to know more. Again no room for wastage, state your strongest reasons why someone may want to find out more.

With news feed ad formats there's an extra opportunity to add in some copy in the "News Feed Link

Description" area, this will enable you to include an additional 200 characters in your ad.

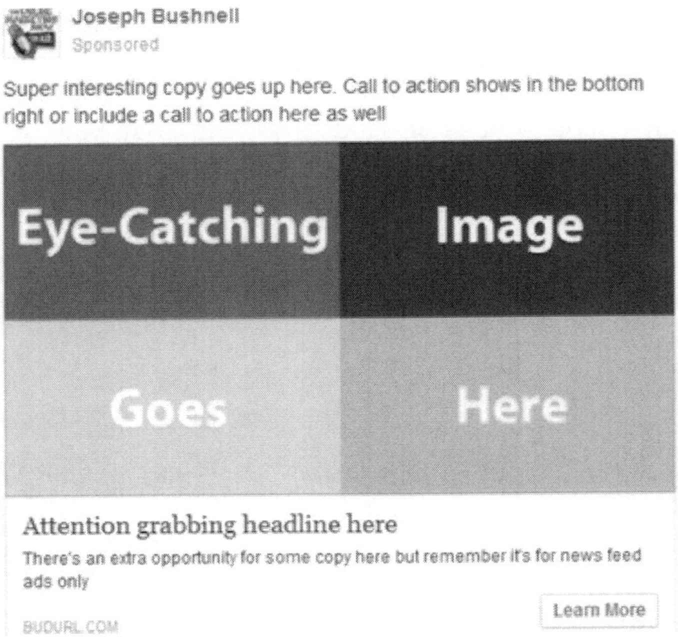

Call to action button

News feed ad formats allow you to place a call to action button on your ad such as "Learn more, Shop Now, Sign Up, Download" but the options are limited. If you find none of them fit your message or if the ad format you are using does not allow you to use a call to action button then you'll need to incorporate your call to action within your copy.

Always include a call to action to let the reader know exactly what they should do next such as... Click here, Register here, Buy here, Click Like, Watch the video etc

Fine-tune Your Targeting

This is the most important part of all. Getting the targeting right is crucial. Even the best written ad with the most amazing image will go totally ignored by the wrong person. You want your ads to be seen by the most targeted prospects possible.

Narrow the targeting of your ad down so that the right people see it...

Location - Do you want people in many different countries to see your ad? Do you want to focus on just one country or maybe a specific region within that country? Maybe you only want to target a certain town or city. All these options are available.

Demographics - There are many options when choosing the demographic you want to aim for including age, gender, languages spoken, relationship & family information, education, work and job information, income and more. There are even some very up to date targeting options in the "life events" category which allow you to target people who have just recently moved house, got a new job or have a birthday or wedding anniversary coming up soon.

Interests - Interests are really important because this is where you can target people based on their personality, the things they think about or care about. It's the psychographics that really matter when it comes to targeting your Facebook ads.

Behaviors - Behavioral targeting allows you to target people based on their spending habits, travel habits, what devices they use for Facebook and much more.

More advanced options for targeting include custom audiences and retargeting so that you can reach people who are *already familiar* with you.

Custom audiences - You can upload your own email database to your Facebook ads account and target your email subscribers through Facebook ads. They might have missed an important email but you can get a second bite of the cherry by showing them an ad whilst they're using Facebook.

Retargeting - Using a retargeting pixel on your website you can recapture the attention of people who visit your website but leave without giving their contact details or making a purchase. This visitor would have been lost without a trace before retargeting technology became available. But now the next time that visitor goes to Facebook they can see your adverts and you can invite them back to your site. Retargeting cannot be done directly through the Facebook ads platform itself so you'll need to use a 3rd party advertising network. My personal recommendation is perfectaudience.com

Now that you have fine-tuned the targeting of your advert, you are ready to publish your ad.

Improve Your Ad Based On Feedback

The last step to winning with Facebook ads is to continually improve and optimize your adverts.

Facebook reward you when your adverts get a good response from their users. If your advert gets a high click through rate (CTR) then they come to the conclusion that your ad must be relevant and of interest to their users and will therefore make it even easier for you to show your ad by reducing your suggested bidding price. This will give you a lower cost per click, giving you the ability to get even more clicks within the same advertising budget.

The opposite is also true. Ads that get a poor response will become more expensive if you want to continue to show them on Facebook.
So it's in your best interest to make sure you don't rest on your laurels, always try to improve your adverts so you get a better response from your target audience meaning you get *more clicks* and spend *less money*.

Split testing different ad variations is a great way to do this. Create multiple ads with different images or different copy and see which gets a better response. Sometimes you'll be surprised at which ads get a better response, you can't always guess correctly. Let your market tell you.

Also try different targeting and see if you can make improvements there too. Look at your reports, they will tell you more about who responded to your advert for example maybe females aged 25-35 responded much higher than females aged 36 and above. Using this information you could narrow your age targeting even further resulting in a more positive response for your advert in the future.

Lastly if you are sending people to a landing page off of Facebook such as an opt-in page or a sales page, split test different variations of those pages to see if you can increase the response in opt-ins or sales that you make. This won't reduce your ad spend like with split testing your ad creative or targeting but will help to increase your return on investment which is the most important statistic of them all.

Optimize in those 3 areas - **Ad creative, Targeting** and **Landing Pages** to make sure that every click, impression and penny counts.

Congratulations you are now well on your way to winning with Facebook ads!

About Joseph Bushnell

Joseph Bushnell is an online marketing consultant who helps business owners devise and execute a profitable online marketing strategy. He is the host of the Online Marketing Show Podcast and writes about marketing topics on his blog over at **josephbushnell.com**

CHAPTER 16

The Real Reason You're Not Getting All The Referrals You Should And How To Finally Fix It This Month

Steve Gordon

Before you jump in, grab a copy of the Free Referrability Assessment at

http://UnstoppableCEO.net/ReferralAssessment

Here's why you should read this chapter: The methods I'm about to share with you produce results...fast. In my own business I have generated as many as 248 referrals in a single week.

More typically, my clients who have applied these methods are often astonished at how immediately and easily they begin to attract 5 or 10 or 20 quality referrals in a single meeting with a client, who had never before referred.

There is a reason you're not getting all the referrals you think you should get. In the next few pages I'll show you what that reason is and what to do to overcome it. Before we get there it's important that you know how I discovered the reason and how it acts as a barrier to a free and abundant flow of referrals.

In 2012, after studying the available wisdom on developing referrals, and after building two businesses on the strength of referrals, I decided to teach a seminar to business owners on cultivating referrals.

It was, as you might imagine, a hot topic. Over the course of several seminars, I taught a few hundred business owners and sales professionals the distilled knowledge about getting more referrals.

All the conventional information boils down to two things:

1. Ask more often.

2. Develop deeper relationships through consistent follow-up.

Both principles are absolutely true, and both work. I've employed them throughout my business-building journey with success.

Several months after my seminars I met individually with 20 attendees. To my great disappointment, none of them had implemented the recommendations I'd taught. And none had seen any improvement in their referral business.

Each person admitted that they believed without a doubt that the actions I'd recommended would help them attract more referral business, yet they'd chosen not to act.

I started to press those I met in later meetings to understand why, if given the solution to their business problem, had they not acted. Again and again, I heard an answer that sounded like this:

"I know it will work, I just don't feel comfortable asking so often. It feels like I'm being greedy. After all, that client just hired me and paid me. And I'm asking for something more. I've done a really good job, and if they appreciate it, they'll tell people."

The bottom line–these business people were avoiding asking for referrals because they felt **uncomfortable.**

They knew they were taking from the relationship and it put them at odds with their normal beliefs and practices.

At the same time, I was a member of, and leader in Business Networking International (BNI)–a strong contact networking group designed to create profitable referral relationships between member businesses.

In this group, members expressed difficulty in finding referrals for other members. Especially in what I call “hard-to-refer” businesses (those that require enormous trust to support a transaction).

As I probed, again the root cause became clear–members were uncomfortable making the referral in those high-trust areas.

So if we know the proven mechanism for getting more referrals (ask more and follow-up to build referral relationships), yet we’re not doing it because it makes us act in conflict with our underlying belief systems (expressed as “being uncomfortable”), how then, can we expect to exert any influence over referrals in our business?

Uncovering The Root Cause

If we deconstruct what happens when a referral is made, it becomes clear why so many otherwise smart business people have such a fundamental problem asking for referrals.

If you and I are friends and I take my wife to a fabulous dinner at a great new restaurant in town, it's easy for me to share that experience with you and refer the restaurant.

For you to go to the restaurant, there's really no risk (sure you might get a meal you don't like, but other than being out $100, there's not much downside). You also know what the buying process will look like when you get there. You'll be seated at a table, be given a menu with prices on it and choose the items you want from the menu without pressure from the waiter (the salesperson).

But let's look at a different type of transaction. Let's imagine that we're again having a friendly conversation and I tell you how pleased I am to have just purchased a $1,000,000 whole life insurance policy. And I tell you that I'd like to introduce you to my life insurance salesperson.

Your reaction (unless you know you have an immediate need for a policy) is to start looking over your shoulder for the door.

And, I've likely put a strain on our relationship. Here's why...

I've asked you to take a sales meeting with a salesperson you do not know. Because I've shared my own satisfaction and joy over buying my $1,000,000 life insurance policy, the implication is that you should want one, too.

If you reject the purchase, you are, in a small way, rejecting me. And you don't want to do that...you don't even want to be in a position to do that. But it goes further.

If you agree to the introduction, you are, in your mind, agreeing to participate in a sales meeting. We both know it. And sales meetings come with sales pressure. You don't want either.

Unless you perceive a real and present need for a life insurance policy you may actually react as though I've overstepped my acceptable social boundary by trying to setup a meeting.

If you think any of this is overblown, think carefully about your own experiences as the referral–the person being referred.
Now, let's look at this dynamic from the side of the referrer–the person making the introduction–in our little scenario, I'm the referrer and you are the referral.

I know that there is great social risk to me in attempting to make this introduction. I already know that you might perceive my gesture as imposing. As the intermediary these are treacherous waters. I have huge downside risk from any number of factors. Yet, the only potential benefit I might receive is increased social capital from the referral and the salesperson, IF the match is a success.

Otherwise, my name is MUD with both of you.

And that brings me back to you, as business person, wanting more referrals, yet too uncomfortable to ask as often as you should.

You know that all of the social dynamic I describe exists and is real. And you know that when you ask a client to give you a referral or make an introduction, you place them in a difficult and uncomfortable position.

So you, and millions of business people like you, avoid the situation all together and simply allow the referrals to happen or not, without your intervention.

A Dangerous Game We Play

Leaving the flow of referrals into your business to chance is a dangerous game. Most often, business owners believe that if they simply provide great service, that referrals will come on their own.

To a degree, that's true. But they often come at such low volume and with such inconsistency that they cannot be relied upon as a primary source of new clients.

Yet, go to virtually any meeting with 2 or more business owners in the room and ask them where they get most of their business and they'll tell you–"word of mouth"–referrals.

Ask the next, more important question: "What are you doing to stimulate referrals?" And most will say, "Nothing."

In fact, in preparation for his book *The Referral Engine*, author John Jantsch surveyed several thousand business owners. He found two things:

1. 63.4% felt that over half of their business came from referrals.

2. 79.9% said they had no system of any kind to generate referrals.

Yet we all know referrals, when they make it to us in the right context, are the best customers. They buy with less effort than prospects that come from cold advertising.

According to a Nielsen study, prospects are four-times more likely to buy when referred.

But only 20% of businesses are doing anything proactive to get more referrals–all because the mechanism for getting them, that has been taught for the last 100 years is based on getting you to do something that makes you uncomfortable.

How To Unlock 10-times More Referrals With One Small Change

So, here we are...we know that referrals represent a MAJOR opportunity for you. And, if you're like the overwhelming majority of business people, the old model of asking for referrals doesn't produce.

Here's how to fix it...

Remove the sales meeting!

Make the first step, the initial interaction something *other than* a 1-on-1 sales meeting with YOU.

Frankly, YOU'RE SCARY!

You might sell me something, take my money...if I end up in a meeting with you (oh my!).

So get rid of all that pressure, on you, on the prospect being referred and on the client or referral partner making the connection. And at the same time, make everyone's life easier.

In place of your sales meeting, instead, place a less frightening interaction...

- A package of information (something that educates *and* pre-sells the prospect on meeting with you)...when you do get to the sales meeting, it'll be FAR EASIER.
- An event, where you can meet dozens of prospects at once...low risk for them and great positioning for you.

- A book (I know, it sounds daunting to create an entire book...I've got clients who have created a book by writing less than 20-pages, in less than two weeks...all beating the pants off of their competition with a few sheets of paper).

Now, my friend, I'm out of space...do read the excellent strategies from my colleagues in this book. Each is a preeminent expert. And, if you'd like to continue our conversation, and deliver a flood of new referrals to your business, I want to make it easy...

About Steve Gordon

Steve Gordon is the Unstoppable CEO. He's on a mission to uncover the traits, behaviors and best practices of *Unstoppable CEOs* around the world...CEOs who are growing their emerging firms despite the challenges they face.

Every weekday Steve publishes quick ideas and tools for CEOs to use and apply in The Unstoppable CEO™ Online.

Because you've read this book, you can get a copy of Steve's bestselling book *Unstoppable Referrals* for just a penny (save $17.94).

Get it here: **UnstoppableCEO.net/PennyReferrals**

CHAPTER 17

Marketing's Missing Link

Ian Brodie

When archaeologists, anthropologists and historians from the 22nd century look back to today for evidence of how we do business they're going to be rather puzzled to find a gaping "missing link" right at the heart of marketing.

They'll find plenty of evidence of "lead generation". When they trace bank accounts they'll spot small fortunes being paid for advertising, websites, SEO, pay per click and a horde of social media experts offering to hook businesses up with potential clients.

They'll see a public being bombarded with marketing messages - up to thousands a day by some accounts. They'll see acres of space in magazines and billboards and hours of time on TV and radio all dedicated to trying to grab the precious attention of customers.

And they'll see plenty of evidence of "selling" too. Meetings, calls, websites, order forms. A huge industry of people teaching others how to "seal the deal" and sharing the secrets of "bare-knuckle selling", "strategic selling", "solution selling, even "sales without selling".

But if these 22nd century historians are business savvy, they'll spot huge gap. A "missing link" that most of today's businesses seem determined to ignore.

The Huge Gap Between Marketing And Sales

Our observers from the future will look at the way most of us do business with puzzled amusement. They'll think to themselves "these 21st century businesses are spending a fortune trying to connect with potential customers. They're geared up to sell to them when the time is right. But what happens in between?"

They'll notice that in the 21st century, just like their own and just like every century that preceded it, customers almost never buy on their very first contact with you.

How many times do you actually have to contact or interact with a customer before they're ready to buy?

There's no single answer, of course. It depends on your industry, your products, the individual customer, their history with you, etc.

But almost without exception, the answer is never "once".

The more expensive, the more complex, the more important, the more risky that the purchase is, and the less that your customer already knows about you; the more it takes before they'll be ready to buy.

According to Brian Carroll, author of *Lead Generation For The Complex Sale*, "Up to 95 percent of qualified prospects on your Web site are there to research and are not yet ready to talk with a sales rep, but as many as 70 percent of them will eventually buy a product from you – or your competitors". <u>If you follow up</u>.

The same is true whether you use networking, direct mail, TV advertising, referrals or social media. It takes multiple contacts to build up the necessary trust and credibility before most clients will be ready to buy.

Most businesses know this, at least intuitively. But what typically happens in practice is that they focus their attention on the glamorous side of marketing and sales. Generating new leads and closing opportunities.

If someone's not ready to buy right now they'll sigh, file away that prospect's business card (never to see the light of day again) and switch to chasing the next "hot prospect". Then the next. Then the next.

Meanwhile, that "not ready to buy" prospect will be getting closer and closer to buying. They'll be getting increasingly frustrated by their problems and beginning to look for a solution.

When they're finally ready, who are they likely to turn to? The business that's kept in touch and had multiple contacts with them, or the one who filed away their card and focused on other hot prospects? Clearly the former.

The Power Of Directed Follow-Up

Nurturing your relationship with a potential client before they're ready to buy is the critical missing link that can make the difference between winning the sale and not. But it's something most businesses either fail to do. Or if they do it, they don't do it strategically.

What they don't realise is that these multiple contacts need to be directed, not just random.

In soccer, the more you pass the ball successfully between your players, the more likely you are to score.

But only if you pass the ball with direction. Your passes have to take you closer to the opponent's net and into danger areas where your players are in a good position to shoot. Just tapping the ball backwards and forwards in your own half gets you nowhere.

Similarly, in marketing it's not just a matter of meeting or speaking to someone multiple times and magically they'll be ready to buy from you. You need to progress your relationship with each interaction.

The CRM Customer Relationship Management (CRM) tools so prevalent in businesses today are brilliant at tracking interactions with potential clients and planning future ones. But planning must be more than setting a date.

You need to understand for each potential client involved in a purchasing decision what they need to *know and feel* to be ready to hire you. And then you need to demonstrate those factors to them through those future interactions.

Let's take a simple example: a leadership coach who's met a potential client executive at an industry conference. From an informal chat, the coach was able to glean that the executive was most worried about the lack of teamwork amongst her senior staff. Not a big enough issue yet that she was looking to hire someone to help. But it was clear to the coach that at some point in the next 3-6 months she could well decide to do something about it.

How should our hero proceed?

Well, first he needs to think through what the executive would need to know and feel to be ready to hire him. It could be she needs to know that coaching is an effective approach for dealing with teamwork issues. Or that other businesses who've used a coach like this have seen their teamwork improve and that's been successfully translated into an improvement in their bottom line.

She probably needs to know that our hero has done this sort of work successfully before and worked with similar teams. And she'd need to feel that she and her team would be able to work well with the coach personally.

Whatever factors he comes up with, he then needs to think about how he can demonstrate them to her in future interactions.

So maybe he could send her an article on the ROI of leadership teamwork coaching that he found in a leading industry magazine. Perhaps an invitation to a presentation he's delivering on teamwork where he uses a number of case studies to illustrate his points (and show his experience). And maybe he can invite her to an upcoming event she'd be interested in where he can chat more informally and build her confidence that the relationship would work.

Of course, you won't be able to work one of your "know and feel" goals into every interaction with a potential client. And you need to allocate your time wisely and focus your best thinking and the most time on the highest potential clients for you.

So the first step in effective follow-up is to make sure you understand enough about your new contacts to decide if and how you'll be following up.

The First Step In Follow-Up: Building Understanding

That means a bit of research. And if your lead generation involves meeting them face to face or over the phone, it means actually listening to them.

It's staggering the number of business people who trot off to networking events or meetings, come back clutching business cards of "leads", and yet don't know the slightest thing about the people they've met.

Because they didn't ask.

So one of your major goals in "live" lead generation is to find out enough about your potential customers to understand what follow-up would be appropriate, and to give you things to follow up on. Because while you want to use that follow-up to demonstrate to them that you're the right person for them to work with, they're only going to pay attention to follow-up that hits the right hot buttons for them. That means it has to relate to the things they care about in business or life.

Armed with your insight on the people you've met you can make a decision about how to follow up.

A System For Follow-Up

There are many sophisticated and complex ways of categorising potential clients. But I find that for most businesses, simplicity drives action. So my advice is to simply categorise your potential clients into As, Bs and Cs.

"As" are the potential clients you think about the most and create tailored plans to nurture your relationship with. They'd be ideal clients for you fitting all your key criteria, and having the potential to bring you plenty of revenue.

"Bs" are the next tier. Perhaps not a great fit on all criteria, or not large enough to warrant a big investment of time. You'll keep in touch with them regularly and expect to pick up some decent business from them. Some of them may become A category clients over time.

C category potential clients are those that you either don't know much about at all, or where it's clear they're probably not going to be a great fit. These are the people you're looking to automate your interactions with, or outsource to others.

How many As, Bs and Cs you have depends on the amount of time you have available for nurturing relationships, and on the nature of your business.

A business-to-business supplier who typically works with a handful of huge clients each year is going to focus on A category clients only.

Someone who sells to a wider market who each make small purchases is going to have a lot of C category prospects they try to keep in touch with in an automated way - for example using email marketing.

And, of course, most businesses will have a balance of each.

After categorising your potential clients, what you need to do is develop a systematic process for managing your keep-in-touch or nurture activities with them.
The key to effective follow-up is to make it value-added to your potential clients.

Most follow-up is all about you getting what you want. Chasing to see if they've made a decision yet. Asking for a meeting to talk about how you could help them.

None of this is valuable to your potential clients. In fact it repels them. Chasing like this makes them dread getting your call and avoid reading your emails.

Instead you want to follow-up in ways that make your potential clients look forward to hearing from you. You want them to tell their assistant to always pass your calls straight through. You want them to open up your emails the minute they receive them.

This will only happen if your follow-up focuses on the things they care about and are interested in.

Yes, you want to demonstrate your credibility and experience to them. At times you may want to remind them of something they committed to do or check on the progress of something.

But the best way to do that is to lead with value first. Give them something useful, interesting or just fun. Then you'll get their attention and your credibility building or progress checking will actually get through.

How do you make sure your follow-up communications are value-added?

You use a process.

Your Day-By-Day Plan For Follow-Up

At minimum, you'll want to make sure you're reviewing your A category prospects on a weekly basis to think about how you could strengthen your relationship with them through value-added communications.

Think about what you know about them. What their big problems, challenges, goals and aspirations are. What they care about. What they fear. What, in their heart of hearts, they'd dearly love to be able to do.

Then think about all the resources at your disposal. What could you do or offer that would help them achieve those goals or solve those problems they're feeling so acutely?

Maybe you've written an article that addresses one of their core concerns. Or maybe you're doing a presentation in a few weeks time on a topic they'd be interested in. Maybe you can introduce them to someone useful, or invite them to an event they'd enjoy.

This sounds difficult on paper. But if you've built a good understanding of what they care about then you will come up with good ideas for value-added follow-up.

Not necessarily every week. But by reviewing every week you'll come up with a lot more ideas than if you just left it to chance.

And by reviewing their details every week then during the week your "antenna" will be much more attuned to other opportunities to add value to them that arise.

With your B category prospects it's a similar process - except you do it monthly.

Automating Your Nurture Process

With your C category prospects, especially if you've got a lot of them, you'll automate the process as much as possible. And the best way to do that is through email marketing.

C category prospects are the folks who sign up for your email newsletter. Or who you offer it to after deciding they're not necessarily going to be a high priority for you (but where they do still hold out potential for the future). To make sure your regular emails to them are valuable, you go through a similar review process. But since you can't do it for them all individually, you identify a single "ideal client persona" to write your emails to.

You try to make that persona as real as possible so you have a picture of them that informs your writing. What kind of job do they have? Are they married? Kids? How did they get to where they are today? What sort of pressures are they under? What targets are they set by their boss? What are the problems and challenges they have to overcome? What are their personal goals and aspirations? Where do they see themselves in 3 years time?

You won't be able to hit the bullseye for everyone. but by doing an ideal client persona you'll be a lot closer to the target for the majority of your potential clients than just shooting arrows randomly.

Your insights into that persona then tell you what you can write in regular emails that they'll want to subscribe to, to open up and to read.

And if you write intelligently you can embed the "know and feel factors" that you need to demonstrate to them in your emails too. Illustrate your value-added emails with examples and stories from your experience so that your readers not only learn, they see the depth of your expertise.

Let your personality come through in your emails so that your readers not only get useful information, they get a sense that they know you and could work with you.

Writing emails like this will allow you to systematically build relationships with large numbers of subscribers in similar fashion to the 1-1 relationships you're building with A and B category prospects.

Building A Database For Follow-Up

If you follow this process of review and value-added follow-up then over time you'll build huge amounts of credibility and trust with potential clients. And because hardly anyone does it, you'll mark yourself out as being significantly different to your competitors.

Over time you'll also build up a growing "database" of follow-up activities.

Chances are that article you sent to John who you met last month might well be useful to Ursula who you met yesterday. Or if not that one, the one you sent to Karen a week before.

Chances are the same set of events and presentations would be valuable to many of your potential clients. After all, as potential clients who are an ideal fit for your services they're bound to share a number of common factors.

After time a pattern will begin to emerge too. Almost a pre-programmed sequence for nurturing. For example:

>> Send link to article on latest industry trends the day after first meeting.

>> Invite to monthly drinks evening with guest speaker the week after.
>> Phone call to ask how they found the event and what they found the most interesting the day after the event.
>> Put article on topic A, B or C in the post a week later.
etc.

Of course, you'll tailor it for individual circumstances. But having a pre-thought through set of follow-up activities for different types of potential clients will not only save you time and effort - it'll make sure it actually gets done.

What Are You Going To Do?

So, the choice is yours.

Do you do what so many businesses do and pump time and money into contacting potential clients, only to switch to chasing the next hot lead if they're not ready yet? Or are you going to make a commitment to nurturing relationships with your best potential clients - either live or via email?

Do that, at it just might be that when the 22nd century researchers dig up your business they shout “Eureka! We’ve finally found the missing link”.

About Ian Brodie

Ian teaches consultants and coaches how to get more clients. He’s been named by Top Sales World Magazine as one of the Top 50 Global Influencers in Marketing and Sales, and raintoday.com named his website at www.ianbrodie.com as one of the “resources of the decade” for professional services marketing.

His Amazon #1 bestselling book Email Persuasion teaches business owners and professionals how to captivate their audience, build authority and generate more sales with Email Marketing.

To get a sample of Ian’s follow-up strategies in action, grab a copy of his “21 Word Email That Can Get You More Clients” at **http://www.ianbrodie.com/21bookgift** and watch what happens next.

CHAPTER 18

Don't Sell! Get Qualified Prospects To Pitch You!

Srikumar Rao

A Vision For You

You wake up in the morning pleasantly charged and brimming with energy. You are well. You ***feel*** *well. You know that you will always be well. You know that you are in the human predicament and stuff will happen. There will be serious illness and death, financial reverses, relationship problems and business setbacks.*

You will deal with each situation as appropriate when it arises but you are anchored in the feeling of wellness. This never deserts you.

Business opportunities arise spontaneously, Customers of the highest quality come to you unbidden. You are at the center of an expanding network of well-connected persons who are all strong supporters.

You are successful in all fields - in business, in civic activity, charitable endeavors and spiritual pursuits. A deep sense of gratitude permeates you and never leaves. What could you possibly have done that you are so bountifully rewarded?

What was your reaction....
...when you read that vision?

Was it incredulity? Was it downright disbelief? Was it a wistful yearning? Was it a 'that would be nice but it will never happen to me?'

A life such as described above is possible. And you can get there. I have helped thousands of persons on all six continents begin the journey. This is a journey that never ends.

You can start today.

Who should read this:
I have a very unusual take on life. And on business.

I will describe this in the next page. If this view resonates with you, then you will benefit greatly from reading the rest of this chapter.

You may also wish to consider enrolling in one of my programs.

If this view does not echo in your very being, then skip to the next chapter.

Or watch a movie. Don't waste your time reading to the end.

My Take On Life

Life is a mystery. We know not whence we came or whither we are going. Billions have come before us and trod the same earth and vanished without a trace. Even the famous and the celebrated have vanished like wraiths leaving faint memories and the residue of their actions.

We, too, will disappear like that one day. Maybe tomorrow. Maybe next week. Maybe in a few decades. We do not know when, but we do know it will happen.

We are a speck of dust on a clod of earth whirling away in the middle of nowhere.

So what do we do in this ephemeral existence?
We work on ourselves. That is the ***only*** thing we ever do in life. We work on ourselves. Some do it consciously. Others do it haphazardly and unknowingly.

Life always teaches us the lesson it wants. The only choice we have is we can learn it easy. Or we can learn it hard.

Everything that we have or know or come across is a tool given to us so we can work on ourselves. *Everything.*

This includes spouse and children and parents and business and physical travails and different forms of benefaction. Equally, you are a tool for the benefit of your spouse, children, customers and others. But that is a different story and we will not enter that narrative.

Your task is to use the tools given to you with as much skill as has been vouchsafed to you.

Your life is a creation. It is a work of art no less than the paintings on the ceiling of the Sistine Chapel or the giant statue of Gomateshwara at Sravanabelgola. You are the artist. All works of art first come into being in the mind of the craftsman.

Use the tools given to you to make the finest creation you possibly can.

My Take On Business

If you are an entrepreneur, then fall on your knees with gratitude. A business is the Swiss Army Knife of all tools. It is a supremely powerful way for you to work on yourself.

You think you started a business to make money or become independent or because you hated your boss or to serve some great purpose.

And now you have to meet payroll and acquire customers and keep them happy and make sure your employees deliver what you promised your customers they would get and deal with interfering government bodies and officials and keep an eye on what your competitors are doing and see if you can somehow placate a family incensed by your absence and desperately keep a semblance of life going.

All true.

But when you are doing all of those things you are also working on yourself. Yes, you are sweet-talking a prospect to acquire her custom, but underneath that, you are developing and projecting your mindset and broadcasting who you really are. The customer interaction is merely a vehicle for your growth.

If this does not make sense to you, then it is time for you to leave and rent the movie we talked about earlier.

Why Are You In Business?

I have asked thousands of entrepreneurs this question.

Most answer along these lines:

1) I don't like working for anyone. I want to be independent (which may be the same thing). I want to make a great deal of money. I like the power of being boss in my little world. And so on.

Fewer answer in this way:

2) There is so much misery of all kinds in the world. I am helping make the world a little bit better in the narrow field I have defined in my business.

And rare is the person who can honestly say:

3) My business is the outward manifestation of the person I am and I work on myself by and when I am working in my business. And on my business.

What Does All This Have To Do With Acquiring Customers And Not Chasing Them?

Actually it has a great deal to do with it. Because what I have put down earlier is the articulation of a mindset. And when you are firmly anchored in that mindset, wonderful things happen outside.

Many decades ago I came across a saying that did not make sense to me at the time. It was, “The Battle of Waterloo was won on the playing fields of Eton.”

It turns out the saying was apocryphal and the Duke of Wellington never really said that but apparently he did remark “There goes the stuff that won Waterloo” when passing a cricket match at Eton decades later.

No matter. The Duke of Wellington himself and many of his officers all went to Eton and it is the attitudes they picked up there that clinched victory at Waterloo. Or so Wellington believed.

I won't comment on the accuracy of that judgment but I will say that, as an entrepreneur, your success will depend largely on what goes on between your ears.

"Wait a minute," you might exclaim. "Business success depends on the actions you take and the environment you face."
And you would be correct.

But the actions you take depend on the way you see the world and this, in turn, affects the environment in which you founder or flourish.

An approach I will share with you is particularly relevant to premium priced services but can be suitably modified for other situations.

It does require you to change how you view the world.

Prospecting, selling and stuff like that
Most consultants I know pride themselves on their ability to do an outstanding job for their clients. Their relationships are excellent and their clients LOVE them.

Most consultants I know do not particularly like the process of acquiring those clients. Their attitude toward prospecting and selling ranges from mild distaste to fierce dislike.

There are good reasons for this. When you ask someone to favor you with his - or her - custom, you become a supplicant. Good consultants generally have big egos and this is jarring.

Second, good prospects have much on their minds and your offering is seldom at the top of the list. So you have to figure out how to woo them. And this is even more jarring.

Finally, a fair number of them will decline for various reasons that have nothing to do with you. So you add rejection to the list of woes and berate yourself for doing something that you shouldn't have or not doing something that you should have.

No wonder you would like to wash your hands off this unsavory part of running your business.

A Different Approach

Now just suppose that you never had to ask anyone for their business. That you could set up your operations such that the best clients vied to get you to accept *them.*

What would your life be like if all you did was work with clients who completely appreciated what you do and were grateful to *be* your clients?

This is not a pipe dream. You can do it and once you determine that you can do it you will find your own unique way to it.

A Shift In Mindset

If you want to get to the stage where clients rush to sign up with you, you have to embrace a completely new paradigm of who you are and what you do. For some, it comes fast. All you need is for this to be explained to you and - bingo! - you adopt it. For others, it may take a long time to jettison long held views to adopt these new ones.

Here are the steps:

1) Be clear in your own mind what you are offering. You are helping your clients become better human beings and supporting them in their evolution to higher consciousness.

Yes, you are providing a service and charging a fee. That is how you make your living. But, underneath that, you are doing what I said above.

There is a famous Buddhist saying, “If the Buddha were a hairdresser, getting a haircut would enlighten you.” Which sums it up beautifully.

Who you are *being* is much more important than what you are *doing*.

Suppose that you received atrocious service at a restaurant where you took an important client. You are upset about it and are talking to the waitress while controlling yourself so you appear poised to your client. What you are being is a sorry individual angry that the universe is not cooperating with him, trying to project an image of coolness that he does not feel in order to impress a client whose opinion he thinks he needs to shape.

What a heavy burden to carry.

Now supposing that you were in the exact same situation but your focus was not on yourself and how it would affect your client and thereby you, but on what could possibly be going on in the life of the waitress.

And you genuinely want to help her through a difficult patch in her life.

You still remonstrate with her about the service, but the 'space' from which you do it is completely different. And, believe me, this is a vast difference and will be noticed.

You are now being a human being devoted to helping others be the best they can be. Some of your clients will sense this and be irresistibly drawn to you and others will be uncomfortable and drift away.

And this is exactly as it should be, because...

2) You need to let go of clients who are not a fit for you in terms of their values and who they are.

We have a tendency to accept clients because they represent revenue and only a fool turns away revenue, right?

I would beg to differ. In fact, I would more than beg. I would do what I could - scold, threaten, blackmail, remonstrate, cajole - to disabuse you of this disastrous notion.

Whether you understand it or not, your problem is not that you don't have 'enough' clients. **Your problem is**

that you spend too much time with prospects and clients who don't deserve you.

Read that again. You need, really need, to spend more time getting rid of prospects - and clients - who are not a complement to your life.

Why what I said earlier is important - more on mindset

How you think about life and business - not intellectually think but what is at the core of who you are - is what shapes how you experience the world.

Here is how many businessmen - or women - view a customer:
1) A necessary evil. She has something you want - think 'money' - so you have to give her something she wants so you can get it. You spend much time and energy trying to figure out how you can reduce what you give her and still get what you want.

Here is how most others view a customer:

2) A being to cherish. You do what you can to make her happy and serve her needs and try to give more than she expects. If you do this, she will give you more of her custom and perhaps even get her friends to do so.

Notice that you are still being transactional. You are doing what you do *because* you want something from her.

Here is how I recommend you view a customer. This happens naturally when you work to adopt the mindset I have laid out:

3) The benevolent universe has sent you the prospect/customer so you can continue to work on yourself. What do you have to learn from this interaction and what value can you give her? You give her value because that is one of the ways in which you work on yourself. And perhaps the best value you can offer is to send her elsewhere because she is not able or ready to appreciate and benefit from what you have to offer.
You can take this attitude because you do not *need* anything from her. Yes, you would like to have an additional customer but you are OK with not having her.

What Happens Next Is Magic

I like Indian food and I have a favorite restaurant. The chef is so good that I can throw darts at the menu from 20 feet, order what was hit and have a great meal. Suppose I went there and ordered 'Chhole Batura'. And the waiter told me that they had, unfortunately, run out.

I have a preference for that dish - in fact I just ordered it because I had that preference. But, since it is unavailable, I happily order another dish and enjoy a fine dinner.

Treat life in exactly the same manner. You *will* have a great dinner. You don't have to do extra-ordinary things to get a particular dish.

My good friend Bill - affectionately known as the Bard of Avon - once remarked jocularly that opportunity knocks but once and you better grab him by the forelock because he is bald behind.

He was dead wrong.

Opportunity is like the subway - or Underground for those of you who live in a confused country that shall be nameless.

If you miss a train, relax and read the newspaper some more. There will be another along shortly.

And as you get to the point where you are *truly* relaxed and ready to read the newspaper some more when you miss a train, things change in your life.

You begin by fits and starts and bits and pieces, to *live* a life like the vision I laid out at the start of this short exposition.

So What Are The Practical Things I Should Do?

I get this question all the time. You, the reader, are impatient and chomping at the bit. "Yes, yes," you mutter - or even shout if your are impolite - "But what do I do next? How do I go about implementing the twaddle you outline?"

Patience!

Inculcating the mindset outlined does not happen overnight, but it can be done with gentle, patient persistence.

I have given you a strategy that is pretty nearly foolproof or as close as possible in this imperfect world we all inhabit. You use *your* ingenuity to translate this into specific activities for your unique circumstances.

That said, here are some general next steps and the attitude underlying each:

1) Come up with something you can give away that conveys tremendous value and also showcases your expertise.

Yes, you do this because you would like it to be a 'hook' that snares many paying customers. But, you also do it because you genuinely want to help others. That is what you were put on earth to do and providing that service is one of the ways in which you work on yourself.

If someone takes your offering and uses it to great effect and never becomes your client or even says 'Thank You', you still rejoice. The fact that what you put out helped another, and countless others through that another, is it's own reward.

2) Evaluate every prospect through the lens of 'Does my heart fill with joy when I get a call from him?' Be wary of those for whom the answer is not an unequivocal 'Yes!' You still wish them well but in a relationship with someone else, not with you.

3) Let them know immediately that they have to try hard if they want to work with you. You have to do this delicately because you don't want to bruise egos but you don't want to cater to those egos either.

There are many ways to send such signals. Here is one that works for me. Anyone who wants to enroll in my capstone program actually has to apply. It is not enough that he/she is ready to make the time and pay the money. They still have to apply and make a case for why they should be admitted and there is a real possibility that they will be denied admission.

I do this because I can weed out persons who, in my judgment, are not ready to engage at the level I expect. I do not want dissatisfied clients. But it also sends a signal that my program is for real and if they wish to take it, then they need to pull up their socks.

I have taught an earlier version at many of the top business schools in the world and mine was the only offering where the students could not decide to take it. They had to individually apply and be accepted. Perversely, or perhaps 'naturally', being accepted into my course became a badge of honor in its own right and many boasted that they 'got into' it.

4) Charge a premium price and bring this up immediately, or very quickly.

Many advise that you should sidestep talking about price till you have firmly established that you are competent and will do an excellent job.

I disagree.

You do not want to be in the business of soliciting clients. You do not want to have to establish your expertise. This is a given.

You want to be in the business of deciding whether the client is good enough for you.

Again, this has to be done delicately but it should be done fast so you don't waste your time. Have you ever courted a 'good' prospect and worked hard to deliver a great proposal and then been told that you were 'too expensive?'

Or, worse, never been told why the prospect did not sign up with you?

Of course you have. Case closed.
How you do this and what you say is a function of your personality and unique to you. But you have to *feel* totally comfortable doing it - otherwise it will not work.

And the only way you *will* be comfortable doing it is if you have adopted the mindsets outlined earlier.

A good way would be to say something like, “I have really enjoyed our conversation, Steve - or Jane! - and would like to explore working together. For an initial project of this type my fees would be in the range of xxxx. I am not sure if your budget will accommodate this. Should we continue talking or should we call it off now?”

Notice what this does:

1) It lays the money squarely on the table and establishes an anchor. Negotiations will then be up and down from this anchor and you have set it high.

2) There was subtle suggestion that perhaps they could not ‘afford’ you. If done right, this leads the prospect to think ‘of course’ they can afford you.

3) There is an explicit suggestion that perhaps you should disengage. This is flat out contradictory to most sales training that emphasizes keeping on talking. Suggesting that perhaps you should terminate engagement conveys confidence and that movement forward will be on your terms.

On with your journey:

Implementing all that I have laid out is not fast. And there will be stumbles as you start walking that path.

But it will lead you to a place where you don't chase customers.

They chase you.

Peace be unto you and yours.

You can download a copy of the syllabus for my program at:

http://tinyurl.com/PersonalMasterSyllabus

If you resonate with what I say and would like to explore working with me, email me at srikumarsrao@gmail.com

Please make a case for why it makes sense for us to work together.

About Srikumar Rao

Srikumar Rao is an author, consultant and TED speaker. His work has been featured in most major business publications in North America and the UK.

He helps entrepreneurs and senior executives make a quantum leap in their life - EVERY aspect of their life. Relationships improve, business flourishes, deep meaning manifests and external accolades shower down.

He shows you how to implement the principles enunciated by the world's greatest Masters to progress spiritually while you prosper materially.

For more information go to
http://www.theraoinstitute.com/

CHAPTER 19

Da Money. Da Marketing. Da Financial Plan.

Justin Krane

I'm really psyched you're here. This book is going to be one of those marketing books that you always keep at your desk, or as a file on your computer.

It's a total keeper, and I'm happy to be able to help you with this marketing and money stuff.

So welcome home! Let's dive in!!!

You're running your business. You want to take your biz to the next level and make more money. Maybe you are spinning your wheels? And getting nowhere quick.

How about the good ol' definition of insanity? Doing the same thing over and over and expecting a different result. More of the same equals more of the same baby.
We've gotta getcha to do some different stuff.

Dah-ling, we gotta get you to do some more mah-keting. You've got to market the shiz out of your biz. . You gotta get your stuff out there. More people need to know what you have to offer.

But this time we are going to bring in da topic of money and mah-keting. Yep. When it comes to laying out an effective marketing plan, one of the most critical things people forget about is the MONEY.

The money is in da marketing. And the marketing is in da money. They go hand in hand.

You must have a financial plan for your marketing - especially the amount of money you want to invest.

You can't go in blind with this money stuff.

You need to be able to back into how much money you can afford to invest in marketing your business.

You need to know where you currently are with your business and personal money. You need to get clear what the current state of your financial situation is.
Once you know your current financial situation, you can make strategic financial marketing decisions - and go to the moon Baby.

As we go through this, I am giving you permission to breathe - and really be ok that you don't have to know everything, or anything, about money. No judging here. This is a safe place for you to tackle this money stuff.

Wherever you are, it's really ok. But it's time to make some progress. I will be right here with you, every step of the way ☺

So let's get to work. Let's roll up our sleeves. Let's make it happen. Let's get wild.

Here's my 6-step process for what goes into that plan:

1. What You Plan On Doing With The Money You Make

Numbers are just numbers. But if you attach meaning to those numbers, you will be more motivated to really dive into this - and finally... create a financial plan.

Ask yourself these questions:

1. How would my future business success affect my personal life?
2. What would I specifically do with the money? What would make me feel really good?
3. Who would I be doing it with?
4. What would it mean to me if I made, hypothetically, $50,000 more in my business?

2. Get To Know The Personal Side Of Your Money

You need to know what your monthly personal expenses are. You need to be able to take out a certain amount of money from your business to pay your personal bills.

Plus, you can't raise the amount of money you spend on marketing (or really anything in else in your biz) if you aren't able to cover your personal monthly bills.

Once you know this monthly personal expense number, you can identify how much money you will need to take out of your business.

There are a many ways you could calculate your personal expenses. You could just make a list of them in Excel. You could just write them down on a legal pad.

Or you could just guess. Wait. No - you really don't want to do that. Get your arms around this number.

You also could use an online app.

I use mint.com. It automatically can do pretty much everything for you. You can link most of your personal bank accounts and credit cards to Mint. Mint then just pulls in all the data for you, and does a decent job categorizing what your expenses are. You may still have to go in and override/adjust a few things, which may be uncategorized. But the heavy lifting is done.

Write down what your monthly personal expenses are here. _______________

Now you need to take taxes into consideration. Ugh!! You thought I would forget!

If you don't factor in taxes, than you will get hit with a big surprise at tax time. And you will have to scramble. Not good.

There are a few ways you can take money out of your business.

1. You can take a draw. That means you just transfer money from your business account to your personal account.

2. You can take a salary. That means you have taxes taken out of your paycheck, and an after tax amount of money gets deposited into your personal account.
3. You can take a combination of draws and a salary.

You need to have a plan on how you will take money from your business, pay taxes, and put the after tax money in your personal account. Review this with your CPA/Accountant.

Part of this tax planning convo with your CPA depends on what type of entity your business is. Some examples of entities are: a sole prop, LLC, partnership, or a corporation.

Write down what your personal expenses are again right here. _______________

Call your accountant and ask him/her what your combined federal and state tax rate is.

Write down your tax rate here. _____________________

Divide your personal expenses by (1- tax rate).

For example, if your personal expenses are $7000, and your tax rate is 35%.

Your pretax amount of money that you need to pull out of your business is:

$7000/(1-.35%) = $10,769.23. So in this example, you would need to pull out $10,769.23 from your business so you could pay your personal bills.

Now, do your own calculation.

____

____

____

Write down how much money you have to pull out of your business pretax so that you can live. Please double-check this pretax number with your accountant.

Now you know how much money you need to take out of your business every month, so you can cover your monthly expenses, and pay your taxes.

3. Cuddle With Your Business Money

You need a system to track your business numbers including: sales, cost of goods sold, expenses (including marketing!), and profits. You need some software that can produce financial reports.

One of best ways to track and analyze your numbers is to use software like Quicken, Freshbooks, or QuickBooks.

If you can afford it, hire a bookkeeper. Let them enter your receipts in for you. Most bookkeepers fees are between $50-125 an hour. If your time is worth more than that, then you need to delegate this. You could be major happy. Like. Big. Time. Happy.

Once you have a financial report like a profit and loss statement, you can start analyzing your numbers. (Getting overwhelmed? Have a glass of wine, and stay with me. You're doing great!)

Make sure marketing is a line item expense in your profit loss (p/l) report. For cash flow and reporting purposes, marketing is a line item expense.

But... keep in the back of your mind that marketing is really an investment. An investment that you want to give you financial results. The money will come back, as long as your marketing is good, among other things.

There are many types of expenses that fall under the category of marketing. Here are just a few:

- Advertising, including Facebook Ads and Google Pay Per Click

- Public relations
- Email marketing provider
- Website expenses
- Coffee/meals for networking
- Employees or vendors (labor) that do marketing for you
- Sponsoring events
- Branding and creative work
- Social media marketing

Print a profit loss report for the last 12 months. Look under the expense area in the report. Find the line that says Marketing.

Write down what you are currently spending on marketing each month. ____________

Nice! You are making some serious progress!!! Giving you a high five.

4. Whatcha Sellin' These Days?

Before you decide how much money you want to invest in marketing, you need to write out a list of your products and/or services. That way, you can forecast how much money you expect to make on your marketing.

Write a list of your products/services along with their prices.

____

____

____

Sweet! There's your list! Feel free to add some new stuff to it!

5. How Much Time Will YOU Spend On Marketing?

Who will do the marketing? You? An employee of yours? Or an outside marketing consultant? Or your grandma?

I believe that you must do some of your own marketing. You can't just outsource it. Some of the marketing needs to be in your own voice.

So...if you are going to be doing any of the marketing, you need to know what your time is worth, on an hourly basis.

Let's calculate this. Stay with me. Breathe. Chill. It's all good!

1. Calculate the number of hours per week you work IN your business. Working with clients, selling your product - whatever it is you do to get paid. Then multiply by 52 to get an annualized number.

For example, if you work 4 days per week delivering your services, and you work 5 hours a day delivering your services, you work 20 hours per week. 20 X 52 = 1040 hours per year.

2. Write down your sales for the past 12 months. For example, let's say your sales are $150,000.
3. Divide your total sales by the # of hours. $150,000/1040 = $144. Now you know what your time is worth, $144 per hour.

You obviously can't do everything yourself in your business. You need to delegate. Now you know if you can find some marketing help for less than $140/hr, it is probably worth it to delegate some of this.

I'm assuming the marketing help is good, and can produce similar or better results than you doing it all by yourself.

Write down what your time is worth.

____

Now that you know what your time is worth, write down how many hours a week you plan on doing your own marketing. Write down the number of days per week as well.

____

6. Determine How Much Money You Plan To Invest In Marketing. Plus, A Little ROI For Ya.

You've calculated your personal expenses. You know how much money you need to pull out of your business pretax.

You have reviewed your profit loss report. You understand where you are spending your money in your business. You have more clarity on your business numbers. You know how much money you are currently spending (investing) in marketing.

You've created your menu of stuff you sell. You also know what your time is worth.

Nice work!!! You are on fiyah!!

Now it's time for you to determine how much money you want to invest in marketing for the next 12 months.

Most people invest 2-3% of their sales in marketing. I'd like you to consider investing 5-15% of your sales in marketing.

Refer back to #3 for some examples of what some hypothetical marketing expenses could be for you.

From a marketing perspective, think about where you want and need to invest in your business.

Make sure you can afford whatever amount of money you invest in marketing.

If you are still not sure what amount you want to invest, that's A- OK. Think about it from a return on investment angle.

Try shooting for a 3X rate of return on your marketing. If you don't think you can make 3 times your money, it might not be a good investment.

For example, if you have $5000 to invest, shoot for $15,000 in sales.

Let's go through some hypothetical examples.

Here's an example where you are investing your time.

Let's say you plan on doing marketing for 8 hours a week. We will stick with the figures we used in #5, where your time is worth $144 an hour. So that's 8X144= $1152 worth of your time for 1 week, or $4608 for the month.

So now you know how much money (really, time) you are investing in this example.
Now you need to think about how much money you plan on making from your marketing time. Let's pretend that you expect to sell widgets at $700 a piece.

In order to get a 3X rate of return on your time, for 1 month, you need to generate $4608 X 3 = $13,824.

That means you would need to sell $13,824/$700 = 19.74 widgets, or 20 widgets for you to make 3 times your money.

Let's use a hypothetical example of investing money, and see what the ROI is on your investment.

Let's pretend that you are a consultant and you plan on doing some advertising. So you do some Facebook ads.

You invest $400 a month on ads, so that's $4800 a year. A 3X return would be $14,400. That's $4800 X 3 = $14,400.

You have 3 packages that you sell to potential clients. All of the packages are annual packages.

Package A = $2500 / year
Package B = $5500 / year
Package C = $8000 / year

You can do the math here to see what different types of packages you would have to sell to generate $14,400 in sales.

Now, it's your turn. Write down the $ amount of money you plan on investing in marketing for the next 12 months.

____

You must be intentional and plan for this.

If you don't know how much money you want to invest, and don't keep track of how much you invest in marketing, how can you be able to measure a return on your investment? And take your biz to the next level?

A Few More Marketing Nuggets

Sometimes you have to plant your marketing seeds, and give them time to grow. Sometimes it will take time for you to make money off of your marketing.

If you are a new business owner, you might not have enough cash flow in your business to wait for financial results (the money) to come in. If that's the case, you want the financial return ASAP, 3 months or less would be ideal.

If you are an established business owner, you will have more time to ride out and wait for a potential return.

So when you make your marketing investments, you MUST think about how long you can wait - financially wait - until you see the money. Some people refer to this as "carrying your investment."

You also need to test and start small with your marketing. That way, if something doesn't work, it's a smaller financial loss. When something does work, you can then make a larger financial investment.

I have created a bunch of tools that you can use to create a financial plan for your marketing.

- Saving Spending Calculator - use this to get a handle on your personal expenses
- ROI Calculator - use this to calculate your potential return on investment
- The Entrepreneur's Savings Planner - Use this to get yourself on a savings plan. Start making your goals a reality
- A 30 minute video of a presentation I gave to business owners about Marketing the Bleep Out of Your Stuff

About Justin Krane

Just go here to download all of these tools for free. I look forward to seeing you there, and wish you all the best with your money and marketing.

http://www.jkrane.com/marketing
Facebook.com/kranefinancialsolutions
Linkedin.com/in/justinkrane

CHAPTER 20

Smart Ways To Track Your Lead Generation Using Google Analytics-For FREE

Vernon Riley

Introduction

Why read this chapter?

This book is full of really smart marketing techniques.

Some are about "what to do", techniques to use, things to do and things to avoid.

Some are about "how to approach marketing".

This chapter is in the "what to do" category. It's all about "how to discover" whether the marketing techniques you pick are working for your business. You can apply this information to each and every lead generation technique in this ebook. As well all the other marketing techniques that you may have tried or try in the future. It will also give you feedback on whether your "approach" is working for your business.

Why do I make such bold claims?

Well, you can only improve lead generation if you commit. But measurement isn't about failure or feeling despondent. Great successes come from incremental improvements. The motor cars that today can do well over 50 miles per gallon are "incremental improvements" on the Model T Ford. The Model T couldn't do much more than 14 miles per gallon. And the good news is that it's much easier to change marketing and web pages than the efficiency of a car engine! (Actually modern cars have many more energy sapping add-ons than the Model Ford - so their efficiency gain is far more than the fuel consumption figures suggest)

So the healthy attitude is to approach marketing as a series of tests. These test not whether a marketing technique CAN WORK.

BUT whether the group people you've chosen (your market segment) are motivated by your message, your choice of media to react positively in the current situation.

The latter is, and should be, a much more nuanced and precise question. A change in any aspect can invalidate the previous result.

So this chapter will show you:

How to measure which of the range of marketing tests you do are resulting in people who react positively to your business.

And start to talk about the profound insights that this gives.

Extra resources are on the web, following the links at the end of this chapter.

How To Think About Google Analytics

Google Analytics (GA) isn't a just website statistics package. Not any more.

Really it's a huge warehouse that can store any data that you wish to collect. And the data collection doesn't have to happen on a web page. Any electronic device on the web can send data to Google Analytics. This chapter considers GA for marketing activities.

GA can store and process this data into useful information. And the GA web pages are a "window onto your information".

Don't be like the people who conclude that GA is useless because they don't see anything useful through their "window". Improve the data and clean the window!

The chances are that problems people have are not with GA. It's because they're not collecting the "right data" for their business. GA is a general purpose tool that CANNOT understand the details of your business. Global Enterprises pay $150,000 per annum to use GA premium. And it's worth knowing that for that money they get consultancy help, a few more facilities and storage of the data quantities appropriate for that size of business alongside all the free facilities we all enjoy. So FREE is a remarkable bargain for the normal micro or small business.

So what should you do?

I recommend you focus on two aspects of data collection:

1. Make sure you've got your links tagged correctly.
2. Set up goals for conversions.

If you do this you'll be ahead of most businesses. Few make GA understand "their business".

If you do this then GA will help you understand where sales qualified leads and customers come from.

Measuring Lead Generation

What is a positive response?

We have to separate useful positive responses from many other activities that are of little or no business value.

A commonly accepted definition of Value is "The amount that someone would pay for something". Using this definition a positive response happens when a visitor "pays" you in some way. For marketers a first "payment" can be some contact details. This is crucial as it allows you (as the marketer) to take the initiative.

I would include the following responses in the list of those that may have little business value:

- Re-tweets.

- Likes on Facebook.
- Sharing a blog post.
- Crawling several web pages.
- Listening to a podcast.
- Becoming a twitter follower.

You'll notice that many of these happen on "social media". They aren't in places that you really "own" or control. They're easy things that people can do. They don't require the individual to identify themselves or make any commitment.

Now they may be helpful to your business and may be a great ego boost. But the business value is open to question. So we should not place much value on them. We need the visitor to make an additional "positive" response.

At a first stage this "positive" response might be:

- Signing up for an offer - giving you contact details
- Responding to an email
- Commenting on content
- Coming to a webinar, teleseminar, teleconference you're running
- Downloading something you've offered in exchange for contact details

- Filling in an enquiry form
- Filling in a survey with some contact details

You'll notice the common theme is the visitor is making a payment in kind that gives value to you ("the marketer"). In most cases - contact details

Once you've got some contact details - you can undertake all kinds of marketing activities to "deepen the relationship".

You'll probably find its better to get contact details progressively. Perhaps try for first name and email address. Then if that worked - offer something else for which you need a physical mail address. Etc etc.

The "conversion process" from visitor into qualified lead and customer may be slow & awkward. But at each stage of the "process" a positive reaction to your marketing means that the relationship is developing. Anything else means that at best things are staying neutral.

So marketing measurement is all about creating positive things for visitors to do. Then we can determine what positive reactions to your marketing are taking place, who is doing it, where they're from etc. etc.

When Positive Response Becomes A Lead?

A positive response doesn't itself necessarily indicate you've got a lead. Businesses will have many different views on what a "lead" is. Many will have a formal process - that is a "gateway" through which a potential prospect has to pass to become a "qualified lead". Qualified leads justify investment of time in the hope of a sale.

Without getting wrapped into the details of what questions need to be answered for "lead qualification"; a few facts are clear.

1. You haven't generated a lead if you can't contact them. So you must have contact details (the positive response referred to above).
2. Asking questions and getting answers is an interactive process that requires contact details.
3. You will have to record (i.e. measure) the answers.
4. Being able to duplicate the "good qualified leads" is an essential part of growing the business.

The last criterion - duplication is a key element most businesses could use help with. And Google Analytics (GA) helps you know where that "qualified lead" came from.

The Information You Need For Lead Duplication

GA considers each visitor is acquired from a source and via a medium. Sometimes they come as result of a particular campaign. Unless visitors are identified (as members) GA treats a visitor as belonging to one device.

The best way to understand how visitors become leads and customers is to look backwards at "where they came from". This is of enormous value, and can tell you:

- How to get more great leads
- How to get more of your best customers
- What pieces of advertising or content were involved.
- What pieces of advertising or content contributed little.

So you should aim to know where all visitors came from. This will then allow you to find out where those who made the positive reaction. In some cases you won't know where the customer first came from. So you have to work at finding out. You do this by:

- Tagging the links (better or for the first time)

- Find reasons to ask (if you ever have the chance)

Source And Medium

GA attempts to intelligently guess source and medium most of the time. Mostly GA gets it right - but sometimes it makes serious errors. GA claims to get unpaid search from all search engines right, referrals from other websites and direct traffic right.
But GA doesn't know whether traffic from facebook is from advertising (i.e. paid) or organic (social media) and tends to classify all the visitors as from "social media". The same is true for many other social media sites that now allow advertising.

Direct visitors often includes respondents to email marketing messages that were deliberately sent. This is because few email clients (outlook etc.) send referral data.

And lots of other cases exist. One that's increasingly important is visitors sent from https (secure) websites to non-secure (http) websites. Referral data isn't sent by default - according to HTTPS "standard" (which is a IETF Request for Comment RFC7321) .

Too few people appreciate that they can tell GA exactly what the source and medium are in every case. And that using campaign further differentiation can be achieved. So all the potential confusion can be removed.

This process can be used for both online and offline links. The offline variant requires a little more work but is very much worthwhile.

Tagging Online Links

In a few cases the links will be labeled automatically. This applies with Google Adwords if you've linked GA and clicked autotagging. It can also apply for some email auto-responders like Get Response if you click the appropriate button. But at the time of writing Aweber and other systems still have to be done manually.

In other cases you may need to label the link manually. The principles aren't hard.

Given a web page, for example :
http://mycompany.com/landingpage
http://mycompany.com/landingpage/
http://mycompany.com/landingpage.htm

You add
?utm_source=<source>&utm_medium=<medium>&utm_campaign=<campaign_name>

Replacing
<source> with the place that you put the link e.g. facebook.com
<medium> with the mechanism that you're using e.g. cpc for cost per click
<campaign>with the name of the campaign.

You can do this manually, BUT for many it's easier to get help (see reference section at the end of this chapter) because :

- You want an easy & complete record of the all the "tags" you've created
- You want to put in the details and cut and paste the result
- You want to do something more intricate

Tagging With URL Shorteners

If you're circulating links on twitter and other online services, you may well find that your links get "shortened". This happens using services such as bit.ly or tiny.url

Now URL shorteners like bit.ly and tiny.url do accept tagged links - and recreate the tags when the link is expanded in practice. This may not be the case for other services. There are now services that allow you to check what you get back with your chosen URL shortener .

Tagging Offline Links

Offline links - in printed adverts, spoken word like Radio can also be tagged (indirectly). But you can't print or say the link with all the stuff GA needs. So you have to be a bit more subtle.

You print or say an alias or "vanity" link. You deliberately setup a redirect so that when the visitor hits this “alias” or “vanity link they get redirected to the actual page you want them to visit. This redirect adds all the tags GA needs to record the source and medium correctly. I created a service to make it much easier to set these up and get them working - if you're not a geek. See the reference section at the end of the chapter.

Visitors Making Many Visits

The smart reader may observe the potential problem with source, medium tagging. What if a visitor comes to your website as a result of a number of differently tagged links. As an example - perhaps the visitor arrives for the first time as the result of an advert. But having signed up for a email newsletter he follows a link and arrives at the website on a number of occasions.

Google Analytics has got this covered using a combination of "attribution modeling" and "multi channel funnels". To be honest it's an advanced technique - and we haven't the time or space to cover here. To read more follow the references at the end of the chapter.

Extra Tags

But that's not all. Alongside these you can also indicate

- Campaign - which marketing campaign this link or article is part of...
- Term - use for paid search that is "keyword orientated"..
- Content - use to differentiate ads or links that point to the same URL

I would advocate using Campaign regularly. Term makes sense if you're using Bing or other paid search - but probably not otherwise. Content is rarer, but could be useful if you were doing split tests and wanted to see the differences in GA

Disappointing or negative responses

Lack of a positive reaction is probably NOT due to the media.

It's far more likely to be due to a combination of:

- A poor message.
- A poor selection of people.
- Poor timing.

And none of these are about the product or service you offer! It's the way you're currently describing it. So your first reaction to a neutral or negative response should be:

- See whether you can change the message
- Change the people whom you have selected should see it/hear it etc.

The Bounce Rate Myth

Bounce rate is commonly misunderstood phrase.

A bounce happens if someone who visits a single web page and exits without going anywhere else on your website. This can be the result of misconfiguration if GA isn't setup to recognize:

- Your website has multiple domains.
- You use a third party shopping cart.

Assuming things are correctly setup. A bounce rate of 60% means that 6 out of every 10 who visited a web page left the site without visiting another page.

But contrary to many bits of hype there is no "right bounce" rate. It depends on what you're trying to do.

Let's suppose you've got a page for people to come and buy a product. And a proportion (say 10%) buy; then you might have a bounce rate of 90% (those that didn't buy). Who is to say that this is less effective for your business than a page where 40% bounce off - but there's nothing for sale on this page or anywhere on the website?

So look at bounce rate; but judge whether it's reasonable in the circumstances for your business!

Setting Up Lead Generation Goals

What's a goal?

In simple terms a goal is something your business wants a visitor to DO. And in the context of this book we're looking to generate leads.

So the next step is to decide what positive response a visitor has to take to indicate clearly that they are a sales lead. You get to choose!

So the options probably include:

- Visiting a particular page (perhaps there is a thankyou page)
- Filling in a form to request something
- Download a white-paper or brochure.

These can be simply set up in Google Analytics.

So the first thing is to make a list of your 5 "business goals", making sure you've got the lead generation goals.

Goals For Your Business

You'll need to create a goal in Google Analytics for each business goal.

At this stage the way your website has been built will have an influence.

In some cases the website will submit forms and have downloads that DON'T CHANGE the page the visitor is on. In these cases the website is probably using something called Ajax. This style of construction will push you toward needing either "event" based goals - or pretending that the visitor action caused a new page to be visited. This latter technique involves creating virtual or fake pageviews in javascript.

In other cases the website will submit forms and have downloads that DO CHANGE the page the visitor is on. Web designers may frown on this and suggest it's not as neat! But upselling and cross selling may be really important for your business - and having a new page on which to do this may be a really good idea!

If you have the choice I would recommend you avoid "Event" based goals to begin with and concentrate on goals where visitors reach a particular page (or virtual pageview) in the case of a download) . Download the resource guide for further clarification of these options here

These are common targets for lead generation.

Now - get one goal setup and check it's working before you try and do more.

How To Setup A Goal

As an example let's suppose you want the visitor to download your brochure - which is a PDF.

Lets suppose this PDF is at
/downloads/company_brochure.pdf

You've got a link on your website to the PDF.

You'll now need to add a small snippet of code to the link because it's a document rather than a real "HTML page" on the website. This code will also need to make sure that the document loads in a new window or tab.

Now each visitor who downloads the brochure will be seen as visiting a "virtual page" named after the brochure.

Go to the Goals Admin area and setup a goal for this virtual page.

You've got a goal setup and can now check it's OK. I'd suggest the following process

a. Open the "Real Time" section in Google Analytics
b. Visit the download page (i.e. the page that has the download link).

c. Check that the overview of activity shows you (your location as a current visitor)
d. Check the "content" show an active user on the "download page"
e. Click the button to make the download
f. Check the conversion shows an active user against the goal you've just setup...

There's video of this process and more details in the resource section at the end of the chapter

Profound Insights From Tagging And Goals

The effect of knowing where visitors come from.
Once you have tagged links all sorts of options become available in GA.

You can look at all the pages - and find out:

- Did some sources and media produce particularly good results in terms of those who stayed and browsed the website? Pick a "second dimension" of source/medium and look at the content pages.
- Whether some sources and media were particularly good at sending people to your landing page?

- Did some campaigns produce people who reacted better to particular pages.
- How do the cost and quality of getting visitors from source and media combination A compare with that from other sources.
- You can create custom segments to see these results side by side.

We've got a set of questions of the type "were some particularly good". We can well ask the corresponding question "were some particularly bad"?

Sometimes the appropriate response to "bad" will be to get stop trying to attract these people. Sometimes you'll want to direct them to different styles of content. This may make a considerable difference.

The Effect Of Setting Up A Goal

Once you've got a goal working in GA even more really useful and interesting information becomes available.

- Firstly GA starts to give you information about your business - not just bland data that could apply to any organization.
- Because the goals are related to your business they help you drive it towards success.

- You can look at the "reverse goal funnel" to see the paths visitors followed before converting (note that in that particular session)
- You can compare how well visitors from different sources perform.
- You can compare how sell different campaigns perform against your goals.

So you can answer questions like:

- Were people from source A more likely to convert than those from source B.
- Which were the best campaigns from an economic point of view

In Conclusion

So we've covered in some detail two aspects of data collection:

1. Making sure you've got your links tagged correctly.
2. Setting up goals for conversions.

If you want help have a look at http://www.roifixer.com/ebextras and the resources section at the end of this chapter

Glossary

Terms

Alias URL: A URL visited with no tags - that applies tags to a 301 redirect.
Attribution Modelling: Working out which source and media where most responsible for a sale or conversion

Auto responder: A system that sends emails at defined intervals. Most operate on the basis of time. Some can use particular events to trigger the sending of email

Bounce Rate: The percentage of visitors who visits a single web page and exits the website without going somewhere else

Channel: A combination of source and medium. This is the same as the general meaning but simply made explicit in terms used by Google Analytics.

Coded URL: Same principle as Alias URL - although the page name is coded rather than being a brand name

Conversion: A positive response where a visitor identifies themselves and takes an action.
Data: The numbers (raw) collected by the web pages and javascript

First party cookie: The standard cookies used by Google Analytics that are only used when the browser hits the website they were created by. Increasingly GA is not reliant on cookies because of privacy concerns

Funnel (Conversion Funnel): A series of pages that leads to a destination goal

GA: Google Analytics

GA Goal: A destination page, time on site, pages per session or event that must happen.

GA Premium:
http://www.google.co.uk/analytics/premium/features.html

Information: Data that has been processed to become useful and meaningful to a particular group of people. Therefore you need to know the audience before you can assert that you have information for them

Javascript: The "programming language" used on the web pages to collect data and send it to Google servers; for use in your Analytics Reports.

Labeling: Same as tagging

Marketing Channel: See Channel

Medium: The mechanism by which the message was delivered to the visitor.

Multi Channel Funnels: A conversion funnel involving a number of different source and media

Organic: The opposite of paid for. Might be social media or elsewhere

Podcast: An audio presentation that can be downloaded. Like a recording of a radio show.

Redirect: A web page that literally "redirects" the viewer to a different page. They are of two types : 301 - permanent or 302 - temporary. 302 isn't much used.

RFC: Request For Comment - the "standards" like system on which the internet is based. Organized by the Internet Engineering Task Force (IETF).

Session: A series of pages on your website visited in succession. In the case of GA if more than 30 minutes elapse between each page, a new session starts.

Source: Where the message was put: e.g. blog

Tagging: Appending ?utm_source etc to a link

Universal Analytics: The latest version of Google Analytics. Recommended since about November 2013. Now does remarketing as well as all the traditional functions
URI: Uniform Resource Identifier. The overall system for identifying where resources are.

URL: Uniform Resource Locator. Includes the domain location and web page address e.g. http://www.roifixer.com/tracker-pro

Vanity URL: Same principle as Alias URL - although the page name is likely to be a brand name

Webinar: Seminar conducted over the web - probably using video and audio

About Vernon Riley

Vernon Riley is a Chartered Engineer with a MEng in Mechanical Engineering and Management from Imperial College London.

Having spent 10 years in complex manufacturing and 15 in software and consultancy he quit corporate life to work for ambitious people who want great results.

He now uses Google Analytics to help Business Owners, Sales & Marketing Directors decide how to spend their marketing cash more effectively. His approach to measurement and tracking draws heavily on engineering by always asking questions like - why do you want to measure that?
He has developed and trademarked the DERIVE process together with proprietary tools to give businesses unique insights into the ways in which they can exploit better marketing tracking in their businesses.

Businesses across the English Speaking World ask for his advice and help.

He operates under two brandnames :
KKSmarts.com
ROIFixer.com.

Vernon is best contacted via LinkedIn
http://uk.linkedin.com/in/vernonriley

Resources
As Google Analytics changes regularly - screenshots haven't been included in this chapter. These together with code samples and other supporting information are all on **http://www.roifixer.com/ebextras**

The resources include:

Tagging Virtual Pageviews - Code samples to download - including jquery and regular javascript versions

Links to URL shorteners & expanders

Multi purpose Tagging Wizard (registration required)

Multi channel Funnels

Attribution modelling
Creating Goals - Screengrabs and videos

Again the link you require is
http://www.roifixer.com/ebextras

CHAPTER 21

The Crucial Step For Achieving Business Success

Laura Ashley-Timms and
Dominic Ashley Timms

Within this book the other authors, have shared a wealth of fantastic information on tactics and strategies to leverage and improve your business success by generating more leads and profitable customers.

This chapter is designed to ensure that *all* your efforts are focused in the right direction. To do that, we want to help you start the process by taking a step back to ensure that you have first developed and refined a clear vision and a strategy for your business as a starting point. This initial step will give you the **framework** in which to quickly implement, in context, all the other strategies shared in this book, so that all of them can build on each other to move your business in the direction you want to take it, quickly and profitably.

The Crucial Step for Achieving Business Success is the single most important factor underpinning the success of every leading entrepreneur.

Rather than just talk theory we will share with you:

- The number one rule that makes you more successful
- Exactly how to define a clear and deliverable vision and a strategy for your business
- The 7 steps to deciding what you really want

We'll also give you an exercise to work through all aspects of your business and identify in detail where you want to take the business and what specific actions you need to take to get you there. The key words here are **'take action'** - this is the one thing that has to happen for you to achieve business success.

Genius Status Is Knowing The Rules

It doesn't matter what business you are in or what stage you are at with running that business, one of the very first things you have to do is figure out what you WANT.

This may sound absurdly simple but it is as true as it is fundamental. You must know where you want to end up because if you don't, any destination will do. What you also have to do is identify what you are doing right now that's working to take you closer to your goal.

Everyone, including you, develops patterns of behaviour that help them be successful; they also have patterns that are less than useful. So the principle is to identify where you are right now and what you are doing that works and doesn't work in relation to achieving the result that you want. We all develop habits, often bad ones, the trick to being incredibly successful is to develop habits that help take us in the direction we want to go. To be more precise the real trick is to develop those habitual ways of *thinking and behaving* so that they feel completely natural and unconscious. This is called the CRUCIAL first step in being successful for good reason because it shapes everything else that follows. It's about developing a new set of rules for how we think.

Think about it in terms of a journey: If you're stuck in traffic or the road is heavy going it's pretty simple to figure out that you might need to take a detour or look for some way around the problems. But what if you're not even on the right road, or you're going in the wrong direction or you're even in the wrong vehicle? You won't notice if your attention's been taken up by the seemingly immediate and important task of defeating the road works or getting past the traffic jam.

Being successful in your business is a lot like winning a game. To win the game you have to know what the rules are before you start or you'll waste a whole heap of time thinking that you're making progress, but in fact you're going nowhere. This point about knowing the rules is very important, if you remember the three dimensional puzzle the Rubik's Cube, some people struggled with it for hours, days, even decades and got extremely frustrated, yet the fascinating thing about that experience is that some people DIDN'T get frustrated or struggle with it at all. They achieved **'genius status'** and were able to get to grips with it relatively quickly and solve the puzzle. The reason they'd been so successful was not because of some great intellect or superior deduction skills. It was in fact just their awareness of the rules. You see every puzzle came with an explanation and a set of rules that needed to be followed in order to win the game. The only difference was the frustrated unsuccessful players had opened the box and got straight on with trying to solve the puzzle. They didn't stop to see what else might be in the packaging. Hence they remained in ignorance and therefore in frustration.

The same can be said for this game of business and indeed... life. There are a set of instructions or rules; a methodology that if you KNOW WHAT THEY ARE can be easily applied. They turn frustration around and make what would otherwise have seemed impossible actually quite simple.

When we don't know what we don't know then there's nothing to question or change. In business we just keep struggling along with the day-to-day problems of everyday life. It's like we're twisting and turning that Rubik's Cube in the hope that THIS TIME will be the right combination; but without knowing the rules it's more likely that we'll never 'solve the puzzle' and achieve business success.

The Number ONE Rule That Can Change Everything

Unlike the printed set that came with the cube, the rules for Business aren't quite as obvious. It's a fact that our human brains didn't come with a set of instructions or rules. They do however exist. There's a set of actions that we can take that harness the unconscious power of the brains we're born with; a set of instructions that can help us complete the game more quickly and more effectively than we're ever likely to achieve without them, which is rule number one.

Rule number one is to realise that what drives our behaviour is our emotion.

Most people (who don't know the rules) assume that it is our intellect that drives us to make the decisions we make - but that just isn't true. Like it or not, it's how you ***feel*** at the time that makes you act in this way or that. The decisions you've taken about how to price your products, how much labour to employ, how much cash to risk or how best to go about your business have not been taken as a result of your intellectual understanding of the situation. They were taken because of how you FELT at the time.

We like to think that emotion is somehow secondary to the decision making process but it's been demonstrated again and again in experimental psychological studies that this just isn't the case. In fact we don't really need the studies to prove it to us. We've all had enough personal experience to show this is true. If you just think back to your decision making process when you bought your last car, no doubt you might have had a bunch of criteria to consider: fuel consumption, number of seats, convertible versus 4x4, parking sensors, on board navigation, the list is endless, but when you made the final choice this would have been more driven more by how the car you chose made you FEEL at the time than just the technical criteria, although you might retrospectively use this reasoning to justify why you bought the particular car that you did! If you don't believe us, examine for a second how you would respond to letting your significant other make the choice for you by providing them just with your key criteria!

Putting this back into a business context, your business functions on decisions; The better and more far reaching the decisions, the better and more effective the business. In the same way that you convinced yourself into accepting that it was your sound intellectual reasoning that made you buy your car; business owners convince themselves that their day-to-day decisions are the best or only ones they could have made. They cite lack of time, pressure or external forces (normally somehow unique to their particular business or industry) that have meant this is the way things are.

It's just NOT TRUE. What's creating their reality is the decisions they are making and what's driving those decisions are the unconscious mechanisms that give rise to our emotions. This is a fundamental rule change from the reality that most people accept.

So What Does This Mean To You, The Business Owner?

Well, the real truth is that if a person takes action to affect their feelings then their decision-making will change. If we take positive and focused action to consistently feel good about moving towards what we really want, then everything begins to take a turn for the better. **You can make more money faster, have more time to do the things you want to do and enjoy the whole process of being a business owner.**

By way of an example we worked with a lady who spent nine years as a reasonably successful interior designer but then rocketed her business to new heights once she figured out what she really wanted and started harnessing her emotions. Whereas once she accepted whatever business came her way and tried to do the best she could with it, she used this technique to think about what she really wanted. As a result she 'laser targeted' her approach towards attracting a particular kind of client and let the others go.

Having worked through this process, she is now more successful (she only works with those who appreciate and can afford her style), more effective (she used her time to streamline her back-of-house processes) and has a far more robust business (she has a solid base, a great niche and a firm financial structure that will weather any national or international financial storm).

So Now You Know Why, HOW Do You Define A Clear And Deliverable Vision And A Strategy For Your Business?

If you're reading this and thinking that you already know what you want from your business then that is OK. What we notice under closer questioning is that more often than not, business owners we talk to are pretty vague...

'I want to be successful'
'I want a strong company'
'I want something to hand over to my kids'
'I want to be profitable'
'I want to be the best in my field'...

These are all laudable aspirations but they don't amount to anything substantial in terms of how our brains operate. The truth is that in most cases it takes some help before a person is able to be really specific about what they want from their business.

We might start by asking questions like why they got into it in the first place... what their initial aspirations were... what excited them about doing what they do... but in the end we have to lead them through a thinking process and a simple exercise before they can finally begin to gain real clarity in their own mind as to what it is they actually want. ***What is absolutely true is that the clearer a person is about what they want, the more likely it is that they will get it.***

The more specifically a person can get into the detail of what success will feel like to them, what it will sound like, how it will smell and taste... i.e. more than just what it will look like, then the more 'distinctions' a person will have defined inside their head. This pre-patterns the brain to recognise these aspects which in turn increases the likelihood that success will be realised.

The unwritten rule, the one that, unlike the Rubik's Cube, did NOT come with the packaging is that ***YOU are responsible for your success in the first instance not by what you do but by what you THINK!***

You might be thinking that we're ignoring the obvious... wouldn't there be some external influence, forcing us constantly to adjust to what's happening around us or in our businesses?

We're not saying that other factors like the external business environment is irrelevant, of course the rest of the world has an effect because it's the world that a person has to interact with. Person A sees the sun and smiles because it's a nice day, Person B grimaces as it's another day that they're having to work rather than play. Yet another person, who sells umbrellas will have a different emotional response again to their friend who sells sunglasses! It's the same day and the same sun but the emotional responses are different because of the meaning each has attributed to sunshine.

If the person who wants more leisure time was clear about what must happen in order for them to be successful enough to gain more control over their time then having a positive outlook and a sunny disposition will probably take them closer to achieving that than the alternative of being miserable.

Clearly that level of awareness isn't there; person A just looks up and smiles whereas person B looks sour. Our point is that it's not the sun that's doing it; it's how they've chosen to FEEL.

Examples of this effect are legion; particularly in sport: there is a particular football team that have an amazing record of conceding goals in the final few minutes of a game. They have had this record for years even though the actual players may have moved on and been replaced many times. Is it just coincidence or is it a negative expectation in the crowd and amongst the players that puts them in an unconscious state of fear during those final few moments...that then so often leads to mistakes and the conceding of a goal?

The players would not even look in this direction. They would blame this or that but the truth is the tiny little decisions that led to their failure were driven by their emotion; THIS is the cause.

By being very specific and imagining the ‘end result’ as if it has already happened you are producing a very specific brain pattern. This becomes a template against which your unconscious can filter everything you come into contact with. The more matches there are, the faster you get to move towards what you want. If you remain unaware of opportunities, those opportunities might as well never have been there. If you don’t know you don’t know. ***If you haven’t patterned your unconscious, you haven’t got anything for it to work with.***

It's Like A Cake...

Recognising that it's not always easy to describe (in the sort of detail we're talking about), exactly what it is that you want - the trick is to break things down into manageable chunks or slices.

There will always be a number of outcomes that you want. In the world of work we can determine these as 'key result areas' within your business. So we slice it up into sections...just like slices of a cake. You just decide what are the key areas relevant to *your* business.

We suggest you focus on the top eight areas. These will vary for every business but the top eight we come across time and time again are:

- Finance and Cashflow
- Strategy
- Sales and Marketing
- Product
- Customers/Clients
- People and Talent
- Production and Processes
- Physical Space

You need to take each area (or slice) in turn, for example starting with the 'Customer' slice and ask yourself what will success in terms of customers in the business look, sound and feel like?

When Is 95% Better Than 100%?

Remember we started by saying that you, the business owner, have to both figure out what you want AND identify what you are doing now that is taking you closer or further away from your goal.

To do this we need to calibrate the degree to which you are happy with each slice of the business, and that's easily done by simply asking the question...on a scale of zero to a 100 (zero being absolute rubbish and 100 the best it could ever be) where are you now with, say, the way your customers respond in your business?

It's useful to remember that in this exercise we aren't worried about what anyone else thinks. This isn't a question of how other people would rate the effectiveness of any particular section of your business. It is a very personal question for you, alone, and it's one of the few times where the most subjective measurement there is (how *you* feel) is actually the most objective measurement we could ever come up with. There's only one person you can never lie to isn't there...and that's yourself. So your feelings of where on that simple scale this particular section is right now is the best measurement there could be.

Once you've given it a number, you need to figure out what would have to be different for that score to be much higher - what would have to change or improve? Personally we're not sure anyone ever gets to 100% (because at around 95% our aspirations rise and we want to recalibrate) so just focus on what it would look like, sound like, feel, taste and even smell like, if the score was at 95%.
So, in the case of the 'Customer' slice, if it was operating at the 95% level, we might want to know:

- What customers are doing now that they weren't doing before?
- What specific customer feedback do you now get at 95%?
- How do customers describe you to other people?
- When you look at the service you deliver, what do you see?
- How do you feel about customer service in your company now?
- How is your customer service different now to when you first did the 'success wheel' exercise?
- What do your customers do now that they would never have done before you reached this level?
- How many customers do you have?

- How often do they refer you?
- What's the main reason they give for doing this?
- What do your customers now look like? How is this different to before?
- Which customers do you no longer service?
- What's the average each customer now spends with you?
- What's the customer journey?
- What is getting them to try your products or services in the first place?
- How long are they staying as customers?
- What percentage are now long-term customers?
- What do you do differently to retain them?
- Which strategies from this book have you implemented to leverage more customers?

Notice that these questions are very specific and they are in the present tense. For this process to work; for the brain to accept something as a reality it must be presented *as if it were real now*. Your brain can't tell the difference between a vividly imagined event and reality. You already know this to be true; any time you see a movie and it makes you jump or you feel like you are part of the car chase; you know that part of your brain is processing this as if it were happening to you, hence you generate the appropriate emotion to go with it.

We can't stress enough that this process is tapping into a natural process that already exists. It's just like the Rubik's Cube; the Cube remains the same whether you read the instructions or not; all that changes when you learn what works, is that you get better and quicker at using it; and it's the same with your own brain.

As you go through each of the key slices or chunks of your business, calibrate them and then describe in detail your 95% *as if it were actually happening right n*ow, then you are starting that patterning process and it WILL lead to improved performance.
That sounds straightforward but how does somebody actually apply a measure to this? We're guessing that for most, this'll be the first time you've thought about these areas in this sort of detail? Remember the measure is entirely personal. It's a huge leap from the way we normally think about measuring performance.

Very often a person will score each of these areas really highly even though they are a million miles away from where they actually want to be. They do this because of the fear of being seen (even by themselves) as somehow not being good enough. Or at the other end of the scale people can score so lowly that they find it almost impossible to imagine what the huge leap to 95% would mean.

In both cases the approach is to take the calibration both literally and gradually. Questions like "What would it look like if you moved up just 2, 3, 4 or 5%?" will usually start the process. Once you start to build this picture you may want to recalibrate where you are now and you will certainly find it within yourself to figure out what you actually want.

It's hugely important to keep away from any barriers or how-to's; at this stage of the process we aren't interested in action planning and we particularly want to avoid jumping into taking action before completing the whole exercise.
It's quite a disciplined approach to work though each of the key segments of the business and detail specifically what the 95% will be like for each. ***The combination of them all will be the ultimate goal for the business owner for their business.*** The process of producing an outcome for each area and committing it to paper is incredibly powerful. It will act like the rudder steering the ship on its journey, or your very own automatic pilot.

Write It Down...In Detail

Just to clarify, you do actually have to write down in detail what 95% looks like for each area of your business and not just a few scratchy lines either! We know that business owners put in all the time, effort and heartache into their businesses because they want something; they want something substantial. So it has to be worth a little effort in detailing what that actually is.

Writing it down allows you to think more positively, both at a conscious and unconscious level. It's often quite hard to get it out of your head and onto paper; once it's done though it makes a <u>huge</u> difference.

People often talk about having the confidence to be a great business person and that somehow a lack of this confidence is what holds them back. Well, another word for confidence is trust. When you trust yourself to do something there's an undeniable confidence that comes with that. The process of thinking something through, committing it to paper and being sure that it generates those feelings of 95% are all about building trust in yourself that THIS IS what you really want. That trust becomes an unconscious confidence and manifests itself to those around you without you necessarily even being aware.

Without this self trust people will revert to what they 'think' they ought to be saying or doing. They will be glib and superficial about what they want and what they think they can achieve.

If we didn't break down the business into its key result areas and then calibrate the responses it would be all too easy for people to respond to questions about what they want with clichés. They will begin to tell you what they think other people see as success rather than what it is they actually want. We've had people tell us that they want millions of pounds and a yacht but then after more detailed discussion told us that the thought of too much money actually scares them and that they hate the ocean!

Each person's success criteria both personally and for their business is unique to them. The goal here is to pattern your 'unconscious pattern matching system' so that your automatic pilot drives you consistently in the best possible way to your desired destination.

Dump The Clichés

The reason that people tend to speak in clichés is because they simply haven't really asked themselves the questions honestly. Clarity and specificity is the key. This is not an exercise for anybody else. It is a highly personal and private activity for you the business owner.

You might well ask "So is that the end of it then, write it down and everything will simply improve - what if the ideas that I've formulated are totally outlandish?"

If they are **genuinely** what you want then this is fine. If it's not really what you want but what you think you should want then it's doomed to failure. Remember the only person you can't lie to is yourself. That's why simple positive thinking on it's own doesn't work; standing in front of the mirror telling yourself that you are lovable and capable when in your heart you know you're an angry axe-wielding murderer just isn't going to do anything! The truth about what you want must be REAL.

One business owner lost everything in a natural disaster; his house, business assets...everything. His 'outlandish' desires were to drive the very best cars, live in luxury and have a life style of international travel that he could increase or decrease the intensity of under his own control. In less than 48 months he had his new Bentley Continental, his house in the country, luxury apartment in the sun and has a thriving business that gives him and his wife all the travel they could ever want. He has those things because he couldn't see anything else in his future BUT them.

As we said at the outset of this chapter, reading this may inform you but all that really matters is ***taking action*** and we want to you to apply this key strategy directly to your business, so get some blank sheets of paper, pour yourself a drink and then complete this exercise for real - and remember ***you've absolutely got to write it down!***

The 7 Steps to Creating Your Habits of Success

You are reading this book because you want to learn how to get leads and drive more profitable customers, at a guess because you want a bigger and more successful business than you have right now. If this is true then taking the time right now to do this exercise will really help you change your actions in all aspects of your business and drive you *only* in the *direction of success*.

To help you with this, in addition to your blank sheet of paper please do ***download the free resources*** we have provided for you, which includes:

- Your Success Action & Wheel Template
- Exercise Instructions
- A set of questions to help you complete your Success Wheel

&

- An MP3 audio track of us discussing this subject with one of our expert team and walking you through the exercise in real time

Go to:

www.Business-Success-Strategies.com/book-gift-crucial-step

to download these **free** resources now

To get to the starting point for this exercise you need to know where you are now.

- Start by drawing a wheel and deciding what the 8 key areas relevant to your business are.

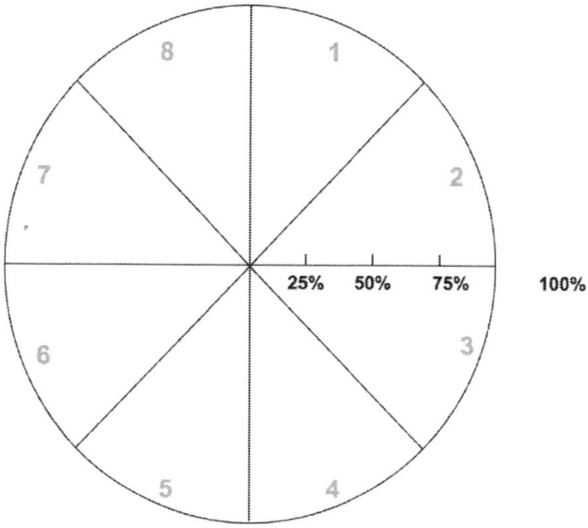

- Write each on it its own slice. They may be variations of the ones on the template - or you may have some completely unique areas that are important to you

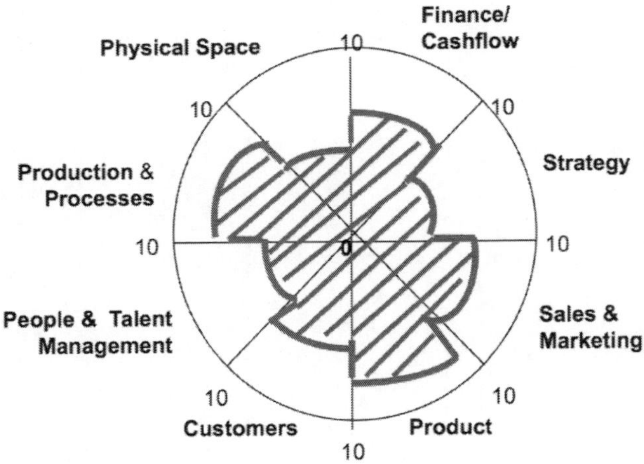

- For each of the 8 areas you have chosen - SCORE yourself between 0-100% of where you are NOW.

At this point you should have something that looks like this:
Then **follow these 7 steps to creating your very own HABITS FOR SUCCESS**.

STEP 1 Start to take control NOW of your future Success - first DECIDE what you REALLY WANT for your business

STEP 2 To make this more achievable - Slice up your Business into 8 BITE-SIZED areas - what are the 8 key areas of your business that you want to focus on?

STEP 3 Now, in the ideal world, what you would like each of these areas to look like? Imagine they were operating at 95% of your "perfect image" - then describe this in detail and WRITE IT DOWN

STEP 4 PUSH AWAY any thoughts or concerns about 'HOW' to get there or 'what the barriers are' or 'why its not possible or unrealistic' - Just define and articulate what you want

STEP 5 For each area, CHECK that what you have written is what YOU REALLY WANT and NOT what you think you 'ought' to want - if these are someone else's "ideals", then redo step 3!

STEP 6 Once completed, check that the overall picture delivers YOUR ASPIRATIONAL BUSINESS (see step 1) - if not then adapt it to meet your real aspirations

STEP 7 Make your desire part of your reality NOW; use reminders, talk about it constantly, SEE IT - make this 7th step your most important new HABIT!

*The free **MP3** will take you through this exercise in much more detail so do download it from this webpage to help you:*

http://www.Business-Success-Strategies.com/book-gift-crucial-step

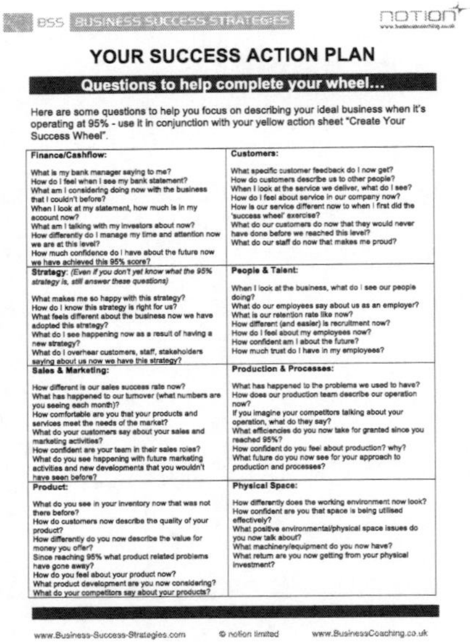

BSS BUSINESS SUCCESS STRATEGIES

notion

YOUR SUCCESS ACTION PLAN

Questions to help complete your wheel...

Here are some questions to help you focus on describing your ideal business when it's operating at 95% - use it in conjunction with your yellow action sheet "Create Your Success Wheel".

Finance/Cashflow: What is my bank manager saying to me? How do I feel when I see my bank statement? What am I considering doing now with the business that I couldn't before? When I look at my statement, how much is in my account now? What am I talking with my investors about now? How differently do I manage my time and attention now we are at this level? How much confidence do I have about the future now we have achieved this 95% score?	**Customers:** What specific customer feedback do I now get? How do customers describe us to other people? When I look at the service we deliver, what do I see? How do I feel about service in our company now? How is our service different now to when I first did the 'success wheel' exercise? What do our customers do now that they would never have done before we reached this level? What do our staff do now that makes me proud?
Strategy: *(Even if you don't yet know what the 95% strategy is, still answer these questions)* What makes me so happy with this strategy? How do I know this strategy is right for us? What feels different about the business now we have adopted this strategy? What do I see happening now as a result of having a new strategy? What do I overhear customers, staff, stakeholders saying about us now we have this strategy?	**People & Talent:** When I look at the business, what do I see our people doing? What do our employees say about us as an employer? What is our retention rate like now? How different (and easier) is recruitment now? How do I feel about my employees now? How confident am I about the future? How much trust do I have in my employees?
Sales & Marketing: How different is our sales success rate now? What has happened to our turnover (what numbers are you seeing each month)? How comfortable are you that your products and services meet the needs of the market? What do your customers say about your sales and marketing activities? How confident are your team in their sales roles? What do you see happening with future marketing activities and new developments that you wouldn't have seen before?	**Production & Processes:** What has happened to the problems we used to have? How does our production team describe our operation now? If you imagine your competitors talking about your operation, what do they say? What efficiencies do you now take for granted since you reached 95%? How confident do you feel about production? why? What future do you now see for your approach to production and processes?
Product: What do you see in your inventory now that was not there before? How do customers now describe the quality of your product? How differently do you now describe the value for money you offer? Since reaching 95% what product related problems have gone away? How do you feel about your product now? What product development are you now considering? What do your competitors say about your products?	**Physical Space:** How differently does the working environment now look? How confident are you that space is being utilised effectively? What positive environmental/physical space issues do you now talk about? What machinery/equipment do you now have? What return are you now getting from your physical investment?

www.Business-Success-Strategies.com © notion limited www.BusinessCoaching.co.uk

And if you need some more help then we have put together a long list of questions you can ask yourself for each of the slices to further stimulate your thinking, which is downloadable from the same webpage.

Once you have worked your way around the wheel you should have created eight paragraphs describing your perfect image of your business.

Now read it though and ask yourself...
"Is this REALLY what I want? Or is it what I think others would want?

If they are someone else's ideal and visions then redo it and adjust it all until it truly reflects what YOU want. Make it really sound like your ASPIRATIONAL business.

Finally, having created this success wheel, are there any little things, some really small quick wins you could actually implement immediately?

We challenge you to find at least ***one action*** you could take today to move you immediately closer to your perfect business...and then ***do it!***

About Laura & Dominic Ashley-Timms

Laura Ashley-Timms started out in international sport and then had a global corporate marketing career before becoming one of the UK's leading Business Coaches who designs large-scale coaching and cultural change programmes for her client organisations.

Dominic Ashley-Timms background in effecting culture change and commercial success through major change programmes during his international consultancy career alongside training up thousands of today's global leaders has given him unique insights into what drives business success.

Together they founded Notion Ltd in 1999 (aka BusinessCoaching.co.uk) which is a leading pragmatic and commercially focused Global Executive Coaching and Coaching Consultancy working with large corporates including Aon Hewitt, EY, Sainsbury's and Vodafone as well as working with MDs and CEOs of fast growth entrepreneurial businesses.

Notion's team have worked with over 110,000 senior leaders and business owners from more than 30 countries, covering just about *every industry and scale of business* and range from members of No. 10 Downing Street to a 'Dragon' from the Den.

As a result of their passion to support entrepreneurs achieve fast business growth they created Business-Success-Strategies.com to bring these resources and coaching skills that were being enjoyed by the top global leaders within reach of *all entrepreneurs*. You can download your free copy of the 'The Crucial Step to Achieving Success' Programme at **www.Business-Success-Strategies.com/book-gift-crucial-step**

CHAPTER 22

Free Resources

Don't forget, at the end of each chapter you can download resources from the person that wrote that chapter. There are some great resources available and you can dig far deeper at no cost.

If you now own this book you are also entitled to register for additional resources. Included are invites to webinars, events and other offers the contributors may make from time to time.

We'll email updates about once a month and will never provide your details to any one else. These updates are also free.

This is how you register:
Go to
http://tinyurl.com/ExtraMarketingResources and complete the subscription box with your name and email address.

Other Resources Available on Amazon .... And Elsewhere

Advertising Secrets: Essential Advertising Tips That Advertising Sales Reps Prefer You NOT To Know (Marketing Magician Practical Guides Book 1)
http://www.amazon.co.uk/dp/B00DY87ZJE/

Are you Ready To Succeed?
http://tinyurl.com/UnconventionalStrategies

Happiness at Work: Be Resilient, Motivated, and Successful - No Matter What
http://tinyurl.com/HappinessAtWorkMotivation

The Personal Mastery Program: Discovering Passion and Purpose in Your Life and Work (CD)
http://tinyurl.com/PersonalMastery

Creativity & Personal Mastery: A program that will profoundly change every aspect of your life
http://tinyurl.com/CreativeMastery

"Creating the Automatic Yes" 4-CD-Set
http://www.altfeld.com/mastery/products/automatic-yes.html

"NLP Skills-Builders" DVD Series

http://www.altfeld.com/mastery/products/sbdvds.html

How to Become a Successful Consultant

http://www.consultingsuccess.com/products/consulting-success-system

Increase your organic traffic to your website and achieve a #1 Ranking In Google's Search Results With Minimal Effort.

http://wallythewebguy.com/seo/

Discover the proven step by step methods used by smart entrepreneurs worldwide to unlock your value and maximize your profits.

http://internetsalesstampede.com/

9464817R10250

Printed in Great Britain
by Amazon.co.uk, Ltd.,
Marston Gate.